OUT
OF THE
DARKNESS

WITHDRAWN

OUT OF THE DARKNESS

From Turmoil to Transformation

STEVE TAYLOR

HAY HOUSE

Australia • Canada • Hong Kong • India
South Africa • United Kingdom • United States

First published and distributed in the United Kingdom by:
Hay House UK Ltd, 292B Kensal Rd, London W10 5BE. Tel.: (44) 20 8962 1230;
Fax: (44) 20 8962 1239. www.hayhouse.co.uk

Published and distributed in the United States of America by:
Hay House, Inc., PO Box 5100, Carlsbad, CA 92018-5100. Tel.: (1) 760 431 7695 or
(800) 654 e5126; Fax: (1) 760 431 6948 or (800) 650 5115. www.hayhouse.com

Published and distributed in Australia by:
Hay House Australia Ltd, 18/36 Ralph St, Alexandria NSW 2015.
Tel.: (61) 2 9669 4299; Fax: (61) 2 9669 4144. www.hayhouse.com.au

Published and distributed in the Republic of South Africa by:
Hay House SA (Pty), Ltd, PO Box 990, Witkoppen 2068. Tel./Fax: (27) 11 467 8904.
www.hayhouse.co.za

Published and distributed in India by:
Hay House Publishers India, Muskaan Complex, Plot No.3, B-2, Vasant Kunj, New Delhi
– 110 070. Tel.: (91) 11 4176 1620; Fax: (91) 11 4176 1630. www.hayhouse.co.in

Distributed in Canada by:
Raincoast 9050 Sh........ ....'ancouver, BC V6P 6E5. Tel.: (1) 604 323 7100;
...... l) 604 323 2600

...ve Taylor, 2011

...he author have been asserted.

The author of this book does not dispense medical advice or prescribe the use of any
technique as a form of treatment for physical or medical problems without the advice
of a physician, either directly or indirectly. The intent of the author is only to offer
information of a general nature to help you in your quest for emotional and spiritual
wellbeing. In the event you use any of the information in this book for yourself, which
is your constitutional right, the author and the publisher assume no responsibility for
your actions.

A catalogue record for this book is available from the British Library.

ISBN 978-1-84850-254-3

Printed and bound in Great Britain by
TJ International, Padstow, Cornwall.

CONTENTS

INTRODUCTION

This is a book about a miracle: the miracle of how psychological turmoil and suffering can bring about spiritual transformation.

Imagine reaching a point where you've lost everything, perhaps as a result of serious illness, depression or addiction. You've lost your career, your spouse or family, your hopes for the future and your self-esteem, and you're so desperate that you don't feel as though you can go on any more. You feel as if you've been completely broken and reduced to nothing.

Or perhaps it's an encounter with death: imagine that you've been told you have a disease such as cancer and may only have a certain amount of time left to live. Everything which has brought you happiness seems to have been taken away. Everything you've worked so hard to build up and everything you've imagined will be in your future dissolves into nothing. There seems to be nothing in front of you except pain, loss and death.

But then a shift occurs inside you. Something gives way; an old self dies and a new one is born. Suddenly you feel a sense of lightness and freedom, as if ties have been cut and weights have been lifted. The world seems a different place, with a new sense of meaning, harmony and beauty. Past and future no longer have any meaning and the worries which filled your mind before no longer matter. All that does matter is the shining 'is-ness' you can see around you and the glorious present that you're living through.

And this isn't just a temporary change. The initial intensity of the experience may fade after a few days, but you're never the same again. You're filled with a permanent sense of well-being and a new appreciation for life. You never take anything for granted ever again – you're permanently aware of the value of life itself, of your friends and family, of the beauty of the world, of your health and freedom. You find yourself no longer trying as hard to make things happen; instead you're content to relax and let events unfold. Your mind is permanently free of worry and anxiety, and rather than spending your life chasing after status, success and wealth, you spend your time trying to help other people or to further your own spiritual development.

This might seem like a fantasy. And it's true that, in most cases, psychological turmoil doesn't have any positive effects. Often we just feel pain, which we want to end as soon as possible. For many people, the process of dying is just full of anguish and sorrow, unredeemed by any sense of freedom or well-being. But for others, intense turmoil is a kind of 'spiritual alchemy', transforming the 'base metal' of suffering into the 'gold' of intense well-being and freedom.

In this book you'll encounter many remarkable people who have undergone this shift: a 60-year-old man who was spiritually reborn after almost dying of a heart attack; a recovering alcoholic who shifted to a permanent state of enlightenment after hitting 'rock bottom' and losing everything; a middle-aged woman who gained powerful spiritual insights through becoming ill with cancer; and a man who became paralysed after falling from a bridge onto a riverbed, struggled for months with pain and despair, then underwent a spiritual rebirth and now lives in a state of permanent bliss.

I became aware of this phenomenon while I was doing the research for my last book, *Waking from Sleep*. While collecting examples of awakening experiences, I came across people who said they had 'woken up' after periods of intense turmoil in their lives. Moreover, these people hadn't just had an awakening *experience*, but had woken up *permanently*. They had never fallen back to sleep. They had a permanent heightened awareness, a sense of connection to nature or the cosmos as a whole, a sense of meaning and purpose, and a permanent inner well-being, free of worry or anxiety. They had attained what the psychologist Abraham Maslow called 'self-actualization' – the highest level of personal development, when a person is completely integrated and perceives reality at its fullest intensity.

Once I began to seek out people who had undergone this transformation, I was amazed at how easily they came to me. Some people replied to a note I put on my website, but others I found by accident – a colleague, one of my students, a friend of a friend, a person I got to know on a course. There was nothing unusual about any of them. Most 'shifters' (as I decided to term them, based on the fact that they had undergone a psychological shift) were fairly 'ordinary' people with normal jobs and families – for example, an architect, an IT developer, a TV writer, a marketing manager, the manager of a heating and plumbing business, the manager of a launderette. Very few of them had known anything about spiritual experiences or spiritual traditions beforehand. (As a result, most of them found it difficult to understand what had happened to them at first.)

I came across so many examples of this transformation that I began to realize that it was much more common than I'd thought. I interviewed 33 shifters in the end, but could easily have spoken to more.[1] People continued to contact me, offering their own experiences of transformation triggered by suffering, but at some point I had to decide that I had enough material. (I've kept the details of all the others who contacted me and plan to interview them at a later date and to include their experiences on a database.)

Some shifters had never talked about their transformation, or had tried to but only met with incomprehension. With this in mind, I'm sure that there are thousands of other people out there who have undergone this experience but never shared it with anyone for fear of being seen as 'weird'. If you're one of them, don't hesitate to contact me through my website (*see Further Information section*).

One purpose of this book is simply to tell the shifters' amazing stories, based on the interviews they gave me. We begin by looking at how psychological turmoil can trigger temporary awakening experiences, then look at permanent transformation through different types of suffering and turmoil in turn, including illness, disability, loss, addiction and general stress, depression and upheaval. All of these can have the same transformative effect. The *source* of the psychological turmoil doesn't seem to be so significant. As long as it's very intense and occurs over a long period, any type of turmoil can lead to permanent awakening.

We will see that some shifters go on to be spiritual teachers. Many modern spiritual teachers, such as Eckhart Tolle, Catherine Ingram and Russel Williams (all of whom I interviewed for this book), have experienced a sudden and dramatic spiritual awakening after a long period of turmoil.

Following this, in the second part of the book, we look specifically at how an encounter with death can bring about this transformation. This can happen through a sudden event, such as a heart attack or a car crash, or, more frequently, when a person learns that they have a chronic illness, such as cancer, and may only have a certain amount of time left to live.

Many people who encounter death in this way experience a spiritual awakening. Even if they know for certain that they're going to die, they experience a powerful sense of well-being. Rather than feeling anxious or bitter – although they may go through an initial stage of this – they accept death and feel a miraculous sense of wholeness and freedom and the glory of living fully in the present. This is such a common response to encounters with death that I have called this section of the book 'Death: The Great Awakener'.

In the third part of the book, I look into the question of *why* these experiences occur. *Why* does suffering have this amazing transformational power? And why do some people undergo this shift while others who experience a similar degree of turmoil or trauma do not?

We will see that one of the most important factors is *letting go*, or detachment. Throughout history, spiritual traditions and teachers have emphasized the importance of becoming psychologically free of attachment to possessions, ambitions and regrets, or to ideas of our own status, success or importance. To some extent, spiritual development is a process of becoming more detached in this way and more self-sufficient and inwardly whole. And it seems that suffering and turmoil can spontaneously generate this state.

Finally, in the last chapter of the book, we look at what this means in terms of our own lives. Do we really need to endure suffering or come close to death to become free, or is there a different route we can take? I will suggest that we can all attain a similar state of awakening without putting ourselves through intense suffering.

For me personally, one of the biggest effects of this book has been to make me realize how common the phenomenon of enlightenment – or permanent wakefulness – actually is. We tend to think of it as something esoteric which only happens to 'special' people – to mystics and gurus, spiritual seekers in India or Tibet. But in actual fact, it's something which happens in everyday life to 'ordinary' people. From my own experience, I would say that it's quite likely that there is an 'awakened' person – probably someone whose awakening was triggered by turmoil – amongst your circle of family, friends, acquaintances and colleagues. Perhaps you're even such a person yourself.

Writing this book has been a massively rewarding experience. It's been a privilege to interview so many amazing, courageous people, who have overcome such massive difficulties and emerged in a new, higher state of being. After every interview I felt inspired for days, filled with a sense of well-being and an awareness of the almost infinite capacity of human beings to transcend suffering and transform themselves. Those feelings returned later, when I transcribed and reread the interviews. I still have them now, when I read the stories – and I hope you will too.

PART I

THE
TRANSFORMATIONAL
POWER OF TURMOIL

1

TEMPORARY
TRANSCENDENCE

Twenty years ago an acquaintance of mine called Tracy was devastated when her partner, the father of her two-year-old daughter, left her suddenly. She arrived home one day to find that he'd taken his money and some of his possessions; he called later that day to say that he was staying with a friend and would call round the following day for a chat. But the next day he called to say that he was abroad and wouldn't be coming back. He said that neither Tracy nor their daughter would ever see him again and that they would be better off without him.

Tracy felt a massive sense of betrayal, together with a terrible sense of loss and separation. She couldn't believe that the man she loved could be so ruthless and cruel. And now that she was a single mother, she felt marginalized and isolated, the scorn of 'respectable' society. On a practical level, she didn't know how she was going to cope. She was a student, her partner had cleared out their bank account and she had a mortgage to pay. She became so anxious that she developed an eating disorder: she started to binge eat, making herself sick afterwards.

After a few weeks, the anxiety and turmoil built up to the point where she started to feel suicidal. One evening, when her daughter was staying with her parents, she found a bottle of sleeping tablets and emptied them into the palm of her hand. Her desire to kill herself was almost overpowering, but every time she moved to take the tablets, the image of her daughter rose up inside her mind and stopped her. She cried for what seemed like hours and eventually fell asleep.

Two or three hours later she woke up in the dark and everything felt completely different. The mental torment had disappeared, for no apparent reason. It had been replaced by a profound sense of peace and well-being. As Tracy described it, 'I felt the most intense love and peace and knew that all was well. Even though it was night, the room was illuminated with light and energy. This light was beautiful and vibrant. It was the most beautiful feeling I've ever had. I felt such peace.'

The experience probably only lasted for a few minutes before she fell asleep again. But when she woke up in the morning, the feeling of dread had disappeared from her stomach and she felt able to cope again: 'I looked around and thought about all the good things in my life and the future. I felt more positive and resilient.'

AWAKENING EXPERIENCES

There are three different types of spiritual alchemy and this is an example of the first type: when turmoil and trauma give rise to temporary 'awakening experiences'. (The two other types, which we'll examine a little later, are when turmoil and trauma give rise to gradual but permanent change and when they give rise to sudden and dramatic transformation.)

From time to time, most of us have experiences when our normal vision of the world is transformed. It could be at the moment of waking up in the morning, while running or swimming, after meditating or doing yoga, or after having sex, but all of a sudden the world seems more real and beautiful than normal. The trees and fields, even the houses and other buildings, seem somehow *alive* and connected to each other, as if they're the expression of a force or energy. You might feel that you're a part of this energy too, rather than separate from your surroundings. And you might feel completely different inside, filled with tremendous serenity or ecstasy and a sense that you have somehow become someone else – a deeper and truer self.

These are what I call 'awakening experiences'. Sometimes they can occur spontaneously, but usually they are induced by different situations and activities. As I showed in my book *Waking from Sleep*, they can occur as a result of physiological changes which disrupt the normal homoeostasis of our bodies and brain. This is why, throughout history, people have used sleep deprivation, fasting, self-inflicted pain and drugs as 'spiritual technologies' to transcend the limits of normal consciousness.

In addition, awakening experiences can occur as a consequence of what I call an 'intensification and stilling of life-energy'. This can happen when we meditate, listen to music, walk in the countryside or just relax. We're removed from the normal energy-draining activities and stimuli of everyday life, and the normal thought-chatter of our mind becomes quiet. New energy floods through our being, intensifying our perceptions and creating a sense of well-being. Our ego boundary becomes softer, so that we are no longer separate and incomplete.

Most paradoxically, however, as Tracy's experience shows, awakening experiences are often induced by states of despair or mental turmoil. Paradoxically, great suffering often gives rise to experiences of great joy and liberation.

In 1969, the biologist Alister Hardy established a Religious Experience Research Unit at Oxford University and began to collect examples of religious or spiritual experiences from members of the public. When he began to analyse the experiences, he found that the most common trigger of them was not – as might be expected – prayer or nature, but 'depression and despair'. He found that 18 per cent of the experiences were apparently triggered by depression and despair, compared to 13 per cent by prayer or meditation and 12 per cent by natural beauty.[1]

I've been collecting examples of awakening experiences myself for almost 15 years, and have found a similar pattern to Hardy. Even now, I'm still surprised at how frequently people send me reports of intense experiences of bliss, harmony and oneness which come to them in the midst of mental turmoil.

Even what seem to be fairly minor episodes of turmoil can give rise to awakening experiences. Here, for example, a student of mine described an experience she had at the age of 15, one summer when she was on holiday in Wales. While walking back from the beach late at night, she had a massive row with her mother that left her feeling angry and frustrated. The problem they'd been arguing about seemed insoluble. As she described it:

Instead of walking back along the road with my mother and sister, I separated myself by walking along the beach, parallel to the road they were on... Suddenly I felt that a great peace had settled inside me. Something magnificent had happened. I felt as if nothing would

*ever upset me again. The world was wonderful. I have
spent my life searching for the feeling again because I
know it's there.*

Similarly, a woman described to me how, as a 17-year-old
girl, she was distraught after splitting up with her boyfriend.
She felt overwhelmed by life and cried for hours, begging
for someone to help her (although she didn't know who).
And, as with Tracy at the beginning of this chapter, when she
woke up the next morning, she was filled with a peace and
contentment she'd never known before:

*I was extremely happy and felt a great love for all
things. It was a very strong feeling, the strength
of which I have never felt before or since. It was
a very sharp contrast to the despair I had felt the
previous night. I felt as though I was filled with love
and compassion. My bedroom looked brighter and
sharper and I remember touching things in my room
whilst feeling a huge feeling of connectedness. I was
conscious of not wanting the feeling to go away. But
unfortunately it didn't last long.*

INTENSE AND PROLONGED SUFFERING

Like the two experiences above, for some people awakening
experiences can occur after fairly short periods of turmoil –
a few minutes or hours, or perhaps a few days. For others,
however, an awakening experience may come after years of
very intense turmoil. And perhaps because the turmoil that
produced them is more intense, these experiences tend to be
more intense.

For example, a correspondent called Emma told
me how, at the age of 20, she was suffering from serious

depression, which was partly the result of her upbringing by an emotionally abusive mother. She became so depressed that she felt suicidal and was hospitalized for several weeks. At one point in hospital, when she hadn't spoken to anybody for four days, she picked up a marble that was lying on her bedside cabinet and started playing with it with her hands, watching it closely. All of a sudden, it was as if the familiar world melted away, to be replaced by a vision of beauty and perfection:

> *I saw reality as simply this perfect one-ness. I felt suddenly removed from everything that was personal. Everything seemed just right. The marble seemed a reflection of the universe. All my 'problems' and my suffering suddenly seemed meaningless, ridiculous, simply a misunderstanding of my true nature and everything around me. There was a feeling of acceptance and oneness. It was a moment of enlightenment. The euphoria and inexplicable rush of 'knowledge and understanding' (it was like suddenly gaining access to a whole new comprehension of what we call 'reality') following this episode lasted for days.*

Although the experience wore off, in a sense it has never left her. It made her aware of a spiritual dimension whose existence she had never suspected and awakened a lifelong interest in self-development. 'In some ways,' she told me, 'I have spent the 25 years since exploring what it meant and how I could perhaps go back there.'

Similarly, a woman called Jill described to me how, over a seven-year period, her whole life broke down. Everything seemed to be stripped away from her:

> *I had studied for a degree, but my career collapsed; I suffered from infertility problems; my partner was an*

alcoholic. I became severely depressed and separated from my friends. Every day I would be in tears and suicide was often in my thoughts. However, I couldn't bring myself to do it, for the sake of my family and dogs, all of whom needed me.

Then one night it happened. The void rolled out completely, the world disappeared and my consciousness expanded into an infinite timeless consciousness which was me, although everyone else at the same time. When I came back to my body, I realized that life was all a dream and not 'real'. I was terrified, although laughing and crying at the same time at this great cosmic 'joke'. I knew what had happened was the pure truth, beyond any question.

Everything shone with a light. I looked at my dog and saw myself looking back and again laughed and cried at the same time. A massive energy pervaded my body, which I couldn't seem to contain.

This is a high-intensity awakening experience, an experience of oneness with the spiritual 'ground' of the universe which is beyond time and space and is the source of everything which exists. And because it was so intense, Jill found it difficult to process. She knew nothing about spiritual traditions or practices and so didn't understand it. She longed for it to happen again, but at the same time was afraid of it. She also felt isolated, because she felt she couldn't explain it to anyone else. As she puts it, 'When I tried to speak about it, everything seemed to be swallowed in a great silence. And even when I could elucidate something, no one seemed to understand. They thought I had cracked up.' (We'll find many similar examples of this incomprehension throughout this book.)

However, after the experience Jill's life gradually became easier. She felt drawn to books about spirituality and eventually began to build up an intellectual framework to help her understand her experience. And over the last two years or so, she has started to have other, less intense spiritual experiences, especially when she's out in nature and can sense what she describes as 'something ancient and indescribable'.

Another example of an awakening experience which came after a long period of turmoil was given by a friend and ex-colleague of mine called David, who was a counsellor at a college where I once taught. He went through a long period of inner turmoil due to confusion about his sexuality. He was married with children, but had always felt sexually attracted to men. Finally he began to realize that he was denying his true self and that he had to come out. And inevitably, as he realized this, his marriage began to break down. However, this turmoil led to an experience of great peace:

> We were on a family holiday in Tunisia and went on an excursion down to the Sahara. We went on a camel ride across part of the desert and at the end of the day I sat on a sand dune watching the sunset. There were quite a few people around, but it was as if everyone else disappeared. Everything just ceased to be. I lost all sense of time. I lost myself. I had a feeling of being totally at one with nature and a massive sense of peace. I was a part of the scene. There was no 'me' any more. I was just sitting there watching the sun set over the desert, aware of the enormity of life, the power of nature, and I never wanted it to end.

PHYSICAL ILLNESS

These experiences can sometimes occur in the midst of *physical* suffering too. A recent student of mine, a middle-aged lady, told me how several years before she had been seriously ill and spent four months in hospital. A lot of the time she was so weak that she couldn't get out of bed, and often felt depressed. However, occasionally this gave way to a powerful sense of serenity:

> The first time I was ill, I was ill for six years and in hospital for four months. Even though I was very ill and in danger of dying, there were times when I didn't feel afraid at all. At times I had a marvellous sense that all was well, that there was a force supporting me, that I was being cradled ... I felt a marvellous sense of well-being. At the time I was religious, and I felt as though God was protecting me.

Another student told me how once she had broken her hip and been confined to a hospital bed for weeks, feeling frustrated and uncomfortable. One day she was lying there when:

> Out of the middle of my forehead intense energy seemed to be flowing out of my third eye. I didn't know if anyone could see it. When my mother came in I felt intense love for her, and it was the same for my friends and family. I felt such intense love and vulnerability. I felt connected to the universe, as if the source of everything was flowing through me.

I had a similar experience a few years ago, just a few months after the birth of our second child. It was a very stressful time, mainly because our baby, Ted, was stubbornly refusing to sleep at night. I also had a heavier workload than normal at the college where I was teaching and a deadline looming for a new book.

All of this stress manifested itself in illness. One morning I woke up and felt as though my throat was wired shut. I couldn't eat or drink and one side of my face had swollen up massively. At hospital, I was told I had quinsy, a complication of acute tonsillitis, and was given intravenous antibiotics, plus a saline drip. The infection had already spread to my neck and chest – which was bright red and swollen – and my bacterial count was very high and kept rising. I also kept getting weaker, until it was difficult to walk more than a few paces.

For the first few days I felt worried and depressed, partly because of the pain and discomfort and partly because it wasn't clear whether the bacterial infection could be kept under control. It was the Christmas holidays and I felt sorry for myself, alone in a hospital bed when I should have been with my wife and children.

But slowly, as I began to adjust to the environment and accept my predicament, a sense of lightness and ease began to fill me. I began to feel a glowing energy inside me, as if I had made contact with a kind of reservoir of well-being which was normally too deep for me to have access to. I spent hours lying on the hospital bed, too weak to read or even watch television, but felt carefree and content. All of the things that had worried me at first – whether I'd have to take time off work, whether I'd be able to finish my book on time – seemed completely meaningless. All of my plans and ambitions for the future and my memories and concerns about the past became meaningless too. Life was pared down to the present moment, the bare fact of being alive at this very moment in this situation. Nothing beyond the moment had any meaning.

I had to have an operation under general anaesthetic, but didn't feel at all worried. When I was lying down waiting to have the anaesthetic, I felt the kind of calmness and serenity that I normally only feel after a deep meditation. I completely accepted whatever was going to happen. I felt connected to something larger than myself, a kind of benevolent force which filled me with reassurance, a sense that 'all was well'.

The operation was successful and the antibiotics began to work on the infection. After two weeks, I was sent home, and the sense of well-being continued over the three weeks it took me to recover fully. And as I realized that I was returning to full health, I also felt a new gratitude and appreciation for my health – for the automatic physiological processes and the energy levels I normally took for granted. It seemed like a miracle just to be alive in a healthy, well-functioning body with enough energy to play with my children, to write, to talk to my wife and friends and meet the tasks of my daily life.

It's true that illness brings a disruption to our normal physiological functioning, so that these experiences could be interpreted as the result of homoeostasis disruption. However, as I noted in *Waking from Sleep*, it's quite rare for illness to generate awakening experiences, probably because when we're ill we're so low on energy and all the energy we do have is channelled into healing ourselves. (Although there are exceptions, such as temporal lobe epilepsy, when seizures are often preceded by intense spiritual and religious feelings.) It's probable that the main factor here isn't the physical suffering itself, but the psychological effects of being ill.

LETTING GO

Experiences like these don't seem to make any sense. How can people who are severely depressed or anxious slip so easily into joy and freedom? How is it possible to move from the deepest turmoil to the highest ecstasy in a moment?

When awakening experiences are induced by meditation or relaxation, they seem to occur in an organic way, but here there's an abrupt shift to a completely different state, one which is almost the polar opposite. Perhaps this is why people sometimes interpret these experiences as being given by the grace of God, especially when they seem to come in response to prayer. The shift from despair to joy seems so abrupt that it seems logical to believe that a higher power – God – has intervened.

However, I don't believe that it's necessary to invoke God as an explanation. I'm going to save a full explanation of these experiences until the final section of this book, but here it's useful to look at how the process of detachment works. Often, when we're depressed or confused and go through major upheaval and turmoil, it's because our *psychological attachments* are broken. The beliefs, hopes, status, success or roles we depend on for our well-being and security have been taken away from us, leaving us feeling broken and empty.

You can see this quite clearly in illness. If you're in a hospital bed for weeks, everything in your life is taken from you. You can't play the roles that normally give you a sense of identity – such as your professional role or your role as a husband or mother – and you lose the status that you normally gain through your job or your social position. At the same time, you might have to let go of your hopes and ambitions, now that you're not in position to try to realize them. And if you're in danger of dying, you have to face the prospect of your *life itself* being taken from you too. In addition to any physical pain you might be feeling, this can cause a lot of psychological pain. (Both of my students who had awakening experiences while they were in hospital experienced this, describing how they felt frustrated and depressed, and I experienced the same when I was ill in hospital too.)

These attachments are the scaffolding that supports the ego – we use them to reinforce our fragile sense of self. And so, when they are broken, the ego breaks down too, in the same way that a fragile building collapses when it's not supported any more. But if we let go and *accept* our predicament, this state can transform from one of desolation to liberation. Rather than a break*down,* you have what might be called a break-*up* – a temporary shift to a higher level of being and a glimpse of the higher self that seems to exist inside us all the time as potential.

Awakening experiences often have long-term effects. Like the woman who argued with her mother on her way back from the beach as a 15-year-old girl, or Emma, people often feel inspired by them for the rest of their lives. They may make us aware of a dimension of reality whose existence we never suspected and awaken an urge for spiritual development, as happened to Jill after her high-intensity awakening experience. Tracy responded in a similar way: she started to read about Buddhism and spirituality and learned to meditate.

Nevertheless, one of the characteristics of awakening experiences is that they are *temporary*. They last for a certain amount of time – anything from a few seconds to a few days – but then fade away. The ego manages to re-form, like a boxer who picks himself up again after being knocked down. The structure of the normal psyche may fade away, but the 'mould' that holds that structure in place is still there, so the psyche grows back into it.

However, we're now going to look at a second type of spiritual alchemy where this doesn't happen. Over a long period of time, turmoil and trauma can 'chisel away' at our normal psyche in such a forceful way that once it has dissolved away, it is never able to reform itself – and the individual experiences a permanent state of wakefulness.

2

GROWTH THROUGH
SUFFERING

It goes almost without saying that the long-term effects of turmoil and trauma are usually profoundly negative. You've probably experienced these in your own life, or at least been aware of them in people close to you – for example, a soldier who has returned from combat and suffers from post-traumatic stress disorder, a woman who has recovered from an episode of cancer but can't sleep at night and feels a constant anxiety that the disease will return, a woman who's been through a painful divorce and feels intense hatred and bitterness to her ex-spouse, or a man who feels depressed after becoming disabled through an accident. As the psychologists Daryl Paulson and Stanley Krippner note, the aftermath of trauma is often 'anxiety that will not subside, depression that will not heal, or psychosomatic injuries that will not mend'.[1]

Another reaction to trauma is dissociation. In order to stop themselves being hurt, some people dissociate themselves from traumatic experiences. They turn off their emotions, make themselves numb and pretend that the experience isn't really happening to them. This strategy is often used by children who are orphaned, prisoners who are tortured or women who are abused by their husbands.[2] Even when the trauma is over, they often remain emotionally numb for the rest of their lives.

A more extreme kind of disassociation is what psychologists call 'dissociative identity disorder', or developing multiple personalities. The personality reacts to trauma by splitting up, as if trying to escape the effects of trauma simply by no longer being there to experience them. This can also be a reaction to childhood trauma: if a child is abused by someone close to them, they may repress their feelings about it, and their memory of it, in order to survive in the relationship, and later these repressed feelings and memories may form a separate personality. Over 100 years ago, the French psychologist Paul Janet described multiple personality disorder as 'the crucial psychological process with which the organism reacts to overwhelming experiences'.[3]

Other people, especially young men, react to trauma by becoming aggressive. The trauma creates frustration and anger inside them, which releases itself as aggression. The aggression can be directed at themselves, expressed as self-hatred and self-harm, or it can be directed at others. That's why children who are physically and emotionally abused by their parents sometimes become aggressive and abusive to their own children.[4] Research has also shown that traumatized people such as refugees are less affectionate and attached to their children. As a result, the trauma is 'transmitted' to their children, and those who don't have stable personalities are more liable to suffer from depression.[5]

POST-TRAUMATIC GROWTH

Terrible though these consequences are, for many people they are balanced by – and even transcended by – long-term positive effects.

In recent years, psychologists have become aware of a phenomenon known as 'post-traumatic growth'. This term was originally coined by the psychologists Richard Tedeschi and Lawrence Calhoun, who interviewed many people who had suffered traumatic life-events such as bereavement, serious illness (such as cancer), house fires, combat and becoming refugees. They found that for many of these people, dealing with this trauma was a powerful spur for personal development. It wasn't just a question of learning to cope with or adjust to negative situations; they actually gained some significant benefits from them. In Tedeschi and Calhoun's terms, they experienced 'positive life changes'. They gained a new inner strength and discovered skills and abilities they never knew they possessed. They became more confident and appreciative of life, particularly of the 'small things' that they used to take for granted. They became more compassionate towards the sufferings of others and more comfortable with intimacy, so that they had deeper and more satisfying relationships. One of the most common changes was that they developed a more philosophical or spiritual attitude to life. Questions of the meaning or purpose of life became more urgent for them. Even if they didn't find hard and fast answers, the search itself gave them a new satisfaction. In Tedeschi and Calhoun's words, their suffering led them to a 'deeper level of awareness'.[6]

Another psychologist, Judith Neal, studied the cases of 40 people who went through post-traumatic growth after life-events such as serious illness, divorce or the loss of a job, as well as near-death experiences. Initially, most of them experienced a 'dark night of the soul', where their previous values were thrown into question and life ceased to have any meaning. After this, they went through a phase of spiritual searching, trying to make sense of what had happened to them and find new values. And finally, once they had found new spiritual principles to live by, they entered a phase of 'spiritual integration', when they applied these new principles. At this point they found new meaning and purpose in life, together with gratitude for being alive, and even for having been through so much turmoil.[7]

In some ways, it seems, suffering can *deepen* us. The German philosopher Friedrich Nietzsche was certainly no stranger to suffering. For most of his life, he suffered from excruciating migraines which left him incapacitated for days, as well as terrible stomach pains. He was forced to retire from his university professorship at the age of 35 due to his ill-health and spent the rest of his life in isolation. He never found a wife or girlfriend, was ostracized by his intellectual peers – because of his unconventional ideas – and had very few friends. He was so unsuccessful as an author that he had to pay for his books to be published, and even then many of them were pulped by the printer. Eventually his writings did begin to filter through to appreciative readers, but by then he was showing signs of mental instability. At the age of 45, he had a complete mental breakdown and spent the last ten years of his life in a catatonic state, living with his mother.

However, Nietzsche had remarkable powers of resilience and always thought that his suffering was beneficial to him. He believed that he was 'more deeply indebted to the hardest years of [his] life than to any others' since his illness had given him a '*higher* kind of health, a sort of health which grows stronger under everything that does not actually kill it!' He saw his suffering as 'the ultimate emancipator of spirit' which was essential for his philosophy, since it 'forces us philosophers to descend into our nethermost depths... I doubt whether such suffering improves a man; but I know that it makes him *deeper*.' His experience was that when a person emerged from episodes of illness, isolation or humiliation, he was 'as though born again, he has a new skin', with a 'finer taste for joyfulness' and an 'innocence in gladness; he is more childish too, and a hundred times more cunning than ever he had been before'.[8] In *The Prophet*, Kahlil Gibran makes a similar point when he writes that 'The deeper that sorrow carves into your being, the more joy you can contain.' [9]

This deepening is perhaps why there seems to be a connection between suffering and creativity. Composers, poets and songwriters often seem to do their best work in response to turbulence. Whereas creative powers sometimes grow dormant when we're comfortable and contented, psychological turmoil can reawaken them. It can break up habitual patterns of thinking and feeling, giving us access to new reserves of insight and vision. This is probably the origin of the myth of the 'tortured artist' – the artist who is unstable and neurotic and flits from deep depression to ecstasy.

It isn't enough *just* to suffer, though – the artist has to work through their suffering and emerge on the other side stronger and more integrated. Great 'tortured artists' like Van Gogh, Dostoyevsky, Schumann or Beethoven weren't just neurotic and depressive – they used their art to help them stabilize and integrate themselves again. Their art enabled them to transcend their suffering, if only temporarily.

A similar thing can happen on a social level. Crisis often creates a spirit of togetherness in communities. Strangers help and empathize with each other and so become bonded. Their shared suffering breaks down their separateness and the whole community shifts to a different level, becoming a real collective entity rather than a collection of individuals. This is why, paradoxically, people often look back at times of crisis with fondness – in the UK, for example, people still talk about the 'spirit of the Blitz' or the 'Dunkirk spirit', not just because these were times when people were courageous, but because they also worked together selflessly and altruistically.

Post-traumatic growth often happens *while* a person is suffering. In that sense the term *'post*-traumatic' is a little misleading. The negative and positive effects often occur at the same time. As well as causing pain, trauma and turmoil can stop us living on the surface of life and open up deeper levels of our being, so that we become fuller and stronger. They can make us more self-sufficient, more deeply rooted in ourselves and less dependent on other people for our well-being. When our life becomes too stable and full of routine, they can jolt us out of our complacency and break up the husk of familiarity which forms over our mind.

The stories we're going to look at now are especially intense examples of this post-traumatic growth.

THE RECOVERING CAREER WOMAN

Cheryl Brown is 50 years old and lives in a small town between Edinburgh and Glasgow. Until two years ago, she was a high-achieving career woman, working as the development officer for a college. She spent her life rushing from appointment to appointment, with scarcely time to think. She was determined to be the best at everything she did, determined to do everything perfectly, and was a hard taskmaster, expecting the same high standards of everyone who worked with her.

However, three years ago, her successful, work-driven life began to unravel due to health problems. She began to suffer acute stomach pain, followed by other problems such as macular degeneration (an eye condition which doesn't normally occur until after the age of 70) and disease of the colon. She felt incredibly tired all the time and was eventually diagnosed with ME, or chronic fatigue syndrome.

She left her job to try to recuperate, but unfortunately her condition hasn't improved. She still suffers from a whole range of symptoms and often only leaves her house twice a week to go shopping. Sometimes she spends the whole day in bed.

At first she found the loss of her independence difficult to cope with. ME is difficult to adapt to, because sometimes you feel better, almost as if you can start your life again. But usually as soon as you do so, the symptoms return and you're thrown off course again. As a result, it's difficult to make plans or to make adjustments to your life. The worst thing, Cheryl says, is the loss of status through not being able to work: 'I've lost all of the things which your work gives – your self-worth and the values that society places in you. I've lost a lot of credibility. That's partly because of ME as well. It's an illness which is not understood. You can look perfectly well but feel terrible.'

But despite these appalling difficulties, there have been positive aspects to Cheryl's illness. It has given her a new ability to live in the present, a new appreciation of life and of the beauty of her surroundings, and a new sense of connection. As she describes it:

It's as if the universe hits you on the back of the head and tells you to stop. I was on a treadmill rushing around, doing a dozen projects at once, and I had to stop.

Having suffered all of these losses, there is not a lot left. With ME, you spend a lot of time doing nothing, because it affects your ability to concentrate. Your cognitive functions are not what they were. It leaves you with a lot of time to do nothing. So I've had a lot of time to reflect and to come to terms with the loss.

All the things that I've lost are connected to the ego. What's left when these things are gone is what's behind the ego. It's an awareness that we're not individuated – that you and I are the same consciousness. I feel like I'm part of something greater than myself.

I wasn't brought up with any religious values, but since my illness I've become aware of something common to all religions, something fundamental, related to goodness and intelligence. It's the universe which we are part of working for the good and the feeling that this illness did happen for a reason.

I've been told not to expect to recover fully, and even if I do I don't want to live at the pace I was before. I'm sure that I can be a force for good by not pushing myself, just by going with the flow.

I feel I'm just beginning on this path and I'll let the universe take me at its own pace. I've come to this realization that striving is not productive – that the more you try to force things, the more damage you do. I actually want my recovery to take longer – I feel as if I'm not quite ready yet.

There are days when I feel absolutely awful, when the pain is unbearable. But that's OK. As long as I accept it, don't try to push it away, then I can get through it.

I think it's made me a better person. It's definitely improved my relationships with other people. When other people are ego-driven, I can spot this rather than react to it. I don't confront them or try to belittle them. I recognize that other people are part of the same substance as me, so I respond with compassion to them.

Now everything seems more real. I go to the country park near where we live and it's been great because I've been watching the trees and the flowers and the birds and squirrels. I've been managing to go out a couple of times a week and I've been watching the seasons change and finding more like a child's view. Days like this are wonderful and I really appreciate the warmth of the sun, even in the winter. Even when it's cloudy and raining, I still think it's beautiful. I feel more of a connection to nature.

It seems to have developed over the past year or so, this heightened awareness and great joy in everything. I appreciate things I used to take for granted. My husband has been wonderful and I'm more aware of the people around me and how fortunate I am to know them.

I also feel that my body has become more sensitive. I became a vegetarian a few months ago and I try to eat organic food and as much raw food as I can. I don't want to put unnatural things in my body or in my house. It's as if through being more connected to things, I've become more aware of the difference between natural and unnatural.

So I don't regret getting ME at all. Something was missing from my life, a sense of meaning, and now I've got it. So to me the illness has been a gift.

THRIVING

Of all diseases, the one that is most likely to bring post-traumatic growth is cancer.

I certainly don't want to suggest that there's anything positive about having cancer; I know many people for whom cancer has just been an intensely painful and miserable experience, as I'm sure you do too. Even after recovery, they don't feel changed for the better, just more vulnerable and anxious. Nevertheless, for some people, cancer certainly can have positive effects. After an initial stage of devastation and anxiety, and despite the pain and discomfort the illness brings, many cancer patients go through a profound journey of self-discovery which changes them radically.

This doesn't just happen once a person has recovered – it can occur while they are still ill, even while they're faced with the possibility of imminent death. Research has found that after being diagnosed with cancer, people gain improved relationships and greater self-confidence, with higher levels of spirituality and appreciation for life.[10] The psychologist Rurhanne Kastner studied a group of breast cancer patients and coined the term 'thriving' to describe their experience of personal development. She found that they lived more authentically, took more responsibility for their own lives and had a more accepting attitude to death and a stronger relationship to the 'divine'.[11]

It's because of this that survivors of cancer sometimes talk about the illness in almost spiritual terms, as a 'great teacher' or even a gift. The famous cyclist Lance Armstrong, who survived testicular cancer at the age of 25, has said that getting cancer was the best thing that ever happened to him. After thinking about little else apart from his sport, he gained a wider perspective and a deeper sense of appreciation. He has said that since having cancer, he cares much less about what people think of him and has become 'more complete, compassionate and more intelligent, and therefore more alive'.[12] He has learned that 'We are much better than we know. We have unrealized capacities that sometimes only emerge in crisis.'[13] Every year, on the anniversary of his cancer diagnosis, he and his wife 'spend that day reminding ourselves to celebrate our existence'.[14]

As late as the 1970s, breast cancer was still a taboo subject in the US. One of the first women to write publicly about the illness was Betty Rolin, an NBC journalist who was diagnosed with it at the age of 29. In her book *First, You Cry*, she writes that 'the source of my happiness was, of all things, cancer – that cancer had everything to do with how good the good parts of my life were'.[15]

Similarly, in her book *The Gift of Cancer: A Call to Awakening*, the breast cancer survivor Anne McNerney writes that 'Cancer is your ticket to your real life. Cancer is your passport to the life you were truly meant to live.' She goes much further than Armstrong or Betty Rolin and even writes that 'Cancer will lead you to God... Cancer is your connection to the divine.'[16]

The connection between suffering and liberation seems paradoxical enough, but these statements seem even more so. To people who have cancer but only experience pain and misery, they probably seem downright bizarre, even offensive. But the next two stories we're going to hear are good illustrations of the transformative power of cancer.

'I WANT MY OLD DAUGHTER BACK'

I recently discovered that a student of mine, Iris, had experienced post-traumatic growth. In fact, as I found out later, that was the very reason why she was a student.

At the end of a lesson one day she said to me, 'Sorry if my essays are all over the place – it's probably because I write poetry.' I asked her how long she'd been writing poetry and she replied, 'It started four years ago, after I was diagnosed with breast cancer.' We both had some free time, so she stayed behind after the lesson and told me how becoming ill with cancer had transformed her.

She told me that as soon as she had been diagnosed with breast cancer she felt like a different person. 'It's weird – you go into the consulting room as one person and you come out of it another one.' She was told she had a very aggressive form of cancer and decided to make changes to her life straightaway, assuming that she didn't have much time left to live. She was a businesswoman, running a car panel company and working six days a week. But straightaway she decided to sell her business.

At first she 'wallowed in a hole of despair. I felt like I was in a vacuum and didn't want to let anyone in. I isolated myself. I didn't want people to come and see me. I didn't even want to see my grandchildren because I thought I was going to die. I thought that if I pulled away they wouldn't miss me as much.' This was when she started writing poetry – angry and bleak poems that reflected her fear.

Shortly after her diagnosis she had a mastectomy and courses of radiotherapy. And to her amazement, only three months later, she was told she no longer had signs of cancer. It hadn't spread to her lymph nodes or to her other breast.

At first she was quite angry – she felt she'd wasted three months wallowing in self-pity, worrying about her children and grandchildren, filled with anxiety and fear. But then she began to feel as though she'd been given a new lease of life. She'd always worried about what other people thought about her, putting more effort into pleasing them than pleasing herself. But now she felt as though she didn't care how she appeared in anyone else's eyes. In the past, she'd never left the house without make-up, but now she stopped wearing it. She decided she was going to live more authentically and do exactly what *she* wanted. She wrote a 'wish list' of all the things she'd wanted to do but never got around to and slowly worked through them: she went skydiving, did a parachute jump, went whitewater rafting and went away for the weekend on her own for the first time.

The downside was that the people around her didn't accept her new self. Her relatives were so used to her giving so much that now they thought she was being selfish. Her mother told her, 'I want my old daughter back.'

Iris felt guilty, but also felt as though she didn't have any choice. 'Your daughter's not coming back,' she replied. 'I'm someone else now.'

After a year, she was told for certain that the cancer had gone. Shortly afterwards, she went to a country park and had what she describes as an 'epiphany': 'The sky was a beautiful blue and I could see all the different leaves on the trees and all the different colours and the grass was different and it was just like everything suddenly came alive again.'

She decided that even though the cancer had gone, she was going to carry on living in this new way. She decided to train to be a counsellor (it was four years later, when she was doing the last year of her counselling training, that I met her). She continued to write poetry, but now the poems were more uplifting, filled with descriptions of the beauty of nature. She wrote poems describing the joy of seeing a rainbow or a waterfall and becoming aware of the preciousness of life. As she writes in one poem, 'Treat every moment as if it is made of gold.'

This has been one of the biggest changes: now she feels that she sees the world in a different way:

> It's completely different. I definitely take in things a lot more. When other people see a bird flying they just think it's a normal thing, but I feel like I see it in perspective, as if it's more real. When I'm out in the countryside and I see animals I feel that I really *see* them. It's difficult to describe, but it's like there's an extra dimension. Water looks different – it's more see-through. When you look at a stream you normally just see the stream moving, but I see the layers of the stream and the flotsam and the tones in between.

In one of her poems, she expresses very vividly how a new dimension of reality has opened up to her:

> The trees of green, of brown, of bare
> That change each season, every year
> Why do I see it now, so clear?
> Why didn't I see it before?
>
> The beat of the wings on birds on high
> The flutter of the leaves that drop
> The shades, the veins, the shapes, the feel
> So different from before.
>
> All the new and different sights to see
> The same, but from a different view.

The other main changes are a new sense of values and a sense of the preciousness of life:

I used to be a bit materialistic – well, it was probably my husband more than me – but now I know that money isn't important, that it's time that really matters. I used to have expensive foreign holidays twice a year, but now I haven't been on a proper holiday for four years and I don't really mind. I'm happy as long as I've got enough money to get by, but I don't need anything else.

I really want to use my time productively. I really want to make the most of life. I wasn't doing that before. I know that time is really precious and that before I wasted it by not really being myself. To waste my time doing something I don't want to do is not a good idea.

Before, she hardly ever spent time alone, but now she enjoys her own company:

The old me tried to avoid being by myself – although I hardly ever got the chance anyway – but now I'm quite happy to do nothing on my own. I'm happy just to sit on my settee, reading or watching a bit of TV, talking to my dog, drinking a bit of wine – and I can really feel fulfilled.

Other people have noticed the change in her too. Her son says she has more of a sense of humour and laughs a lot more now, while her brother says she's like she was as a girl, more carefree and relaxed and less stressed.

However, although she is happier in most ways, Iris told me that there have been some downsides to her experience. She feels insecure because of the changes to her body and finds it difficult to get into relationships. She feels less trusting of people, partly because she's never sure of how they will react when she tells them about having cancer. Nevertheless, she feels that becoming ill with cancer was a 'massive life-changing experience which has woken me up and given me a new life'.

CARRIE'S EXPERIENCE OF THRIVING

One woman who has been through a very powerful process of 'thriving' – to an even greater degree than Iris – is a television writer named Carrie Mitchell, who lives in Yorkshire and is in her early forties. She was diagnosed with breast cancer in September 2007, but even before then she had been through a great deal of suffering and trauma. When she was a young child, her younger sister died at the age of six. She became ill one night and died the following morning, in their mother's arms, from viral meningitis. Their mother was completely devastated; she broke down in front of Carrie and was never the same person again.

Carrie didn't realize how affected she had been by this bereavement until 30 years later, when there was another death in the family. This was her nephew, who had been born prematurely and always had breathing difficulties. At the age of 18 months, he caught a chest infection and spent months in hospital, with his life in danger. Carrie was very close to her sister and her family, and visited her nephew almost every day, often staying overnight. When he died, she had grief therapy for more than a year, which also helped her to come to terms with the loss of her younger sister.

Her nephew's illness also had terrible consequences for the health of her sister, who was diabetic. Inevitably, as she was so preoccupied with the welfare of her son, she neglected her own health, and developed an eye condition which led to her becoming blind. She lost her sight within five months and also suffered serious heart and kidney problems. She had to have kidney dialysis three or four times a week for 18 months, until she had a double heart and kidney transplant.

Carrie was looking after her sister – she drove her to hospital for dialysis three times a week – and trying to lead her own life at the same time. Before this trauma, she'd been leading what she calls a 'consumerist' lifestyle. She had made a lot of money writing soap opera episodes for TV and felt obliged to spend it. As she describes it, 'I bought my own house and got caught up in the whole thing of buying stuff I didn't really need and filled my house with furniture and all kinds of "nice" things.'

But now she started to feel disconnected, as if her life didn't have any meaning any more. Her bank balance kept increasing, but she stopped spending her money. She was suffering from depression – although she didn't realize it at the time – and threw herself into work as a way of anaesthetizing herself to the pain. As she describes it, 'I just lived in this fictional world of soap-opera characters and tried to forget about everything else.'

On a visit to her bereavement therapist, Carrie told her that she felt completely broken. She said she had lost all ambition and all interest in the world around her, and that it was as if she was looking at the world though a window. And then, just a few days later, she was diagnosed with breast cancer.

It was a massive shock, partly because in her family she'd always been the person who didn't get ill, the person who cared for everyone else. It was a role reversal: she lived on her own and now she needed her parents to be there for her, instead of the other way round. She was told that her cancer was an aggressive one which had already spread to one lymph node. She was devastated and scared. 'It confirmed my fears that my family was doomed,' she told me. 'I thought it was another terrible tragedy that my mother was going to suffer.'

After being diagnosed, she wanted to know why she'd got cancer. She didn't fit any of the normal criteria – she wasn't overweight, didn't drink too much and didn't have a bad diet – so why had her body decided to malfunction? She started to read books about healing and the link between the mind and body. She read a book which said that cancer was often the consequence of a lot of unresolved emotional sadness. She thought this applied to her – she had been carrying around stress and trauma inside her body since she was six years old. She decided that if she wanted to heal herself she would have to deal with this stress and trauma. So she decided to address what was happening to her emotionally.

She started to meditate regularly and began to feel the benefits straightaway. She found that by keeping herself calm through meditation she could create a more positive attitude. She did a lot of relaxation exercises too, and positive visualizations, along with having chemotherapy and radiotherapy. And after a year she was told that there was no more cancer in her body.

Now Carrie is technically in remission, even though she has to take medication for another five years. And, like Iris, she is now a different person:

> I've had a weird but wonderful journey, hitting rock bottom and going back up again. It's quite amazing how things have turned around. It's been very liberating, and led to a massive change in my values and my ambitions. I feel as if I've woken up to something.

I used to be really ambitious – I used to really want to write a soap that won a BAFTA – but now I don't want to win an award for anything. I'm interested in living as harmonious and peaceful a life as possible.

Now I feel as if I'm rejecting material things too. I'm backtracking. I've got a big house, but I'm going to put it on the market soon. I'm not interested in the idea of having a mortgage. I'm questioning a lot of things like that. I used to spend a lot of time passively watching TV, but I don't do that any more. It's got to the point now where I don't feel comfortable writing soaps, because I don't want to perpetuate them. I feel like I'm peddling misery and want to do something more positive.

I have a completely different attitude to nature. I walk every day with my dog, but before I would think of it as a chore, whereas now it's the best part of my day. After my diagnosis I went to Cornwall for six months and I just spent the whole time by the sea. I felt a really strong connection with nature, feeling a part of it for the first time ever. It felt joyous to be outside.

Now I live very much in the present. When you have a realization of what really matters, it stops you getting lost in negative thoughts, which I used to do. I'm always reminded of how lucky I am. And that helps me to enjoy things for what they are. If I'm with friends and I catch myself thinking about something else, I can bring myself back to the present. Before, I'd just follow my thoughts. And because I'm more present with other people, I'm connecting with them more. They've responded to the change in me and become more present as well. So my relationships have definitely improved.

When you've been really low, everything is good in comparison. I feel a lot freer, a lot less encumbered by anxiety and fear of death. When I was diagnosed, I was terrified of death. I don't think I'm completely free of it, but I feel much more connected to a wider whole, as an ongoing process of life and rebirth, so the fear has almost gone. I've had enough of suffering and being caught up in negative thought patterns. I've let go of them. If you live in the moment, you realize that there's no point projecting into the future. Whatever happens is going to happen, so there's no point worrying about it. You just have to accept it. Even if the worst happens, I know I will get through it.

I'm very much aware that I used to live a very ego-based kind of life and I feel that through being aware of it, I can drop it. Now I see myself as part of a whole. I see my life in a universal context, whereas before I didn't think beyond my own desires.

If this is what having all these traumas has led to, then I guess I'm very lucky I've emerged from the experience a rather different, more 'evolved' spiritual person.

The only negative side to Carrie's experience is that, as Iris also found, her transformation has created a distance between her and her family and old friends. It may take some time for them to fully understand or accept her new self.

Cheryl, Iris and Carrie have all transformed in very similar ways: they have all felt reborn, as if they have been given a new lease of life. They have all found a new contentment and meaning, including a new appreciation of the fact of being alive, and of the 'small things' they used to take for granted. They have become less materialistic and ambitious, and now feel a sense of connection to something larger than themselves. They no longer experience life as an isolated ego, separate from a world 'out there'. Carrie mentions that she feels a new connection to nature, while Cheryl describes her awareness that 'You and I are the same consciousness. I feel like I'm part of something greater than myself.' In addition, they have all learned to 'step back', to stop striving and *allow* things to happen, trusting in the future rather than worrying about it. Perhaps most significantly, though, they have all gained a new perception of reality. The world has become a much more real and beautiful place to them. As Iris describes it vividly, 'When I'm out in the countryside and I see animals I feel that I *really* see them.'

I'm going to save my full discussion of the reasons for this transformation for the final section of this book, but at this stage it's perhaps worth highlighting the importance of *attention*. One of the reasons why Cheryl, Iris and Carrie have 'woken up' to the is-ness and beauty of the world is simply because they now pay more attention to it. For Cheryl this is because she is no longer so immersed in her job and so busy rushing from one task to the next; she has slowed down and learned to focus on the present moment and her immediate surroundings. In a similar way, Carrie has learned to live in the present rather than to distract herself through writing or to focus on her future ambitions. She has also become less immersed in her own thoughts and so more attentive to her surroundings and her experiences.

An important part of Iris and Carrie's experiences in particular is that they were told they might only have a certain amount of time left to live. As well as suffering the trauma of illness itself, they had to face possible death. As we'll see later, becoming intensely aware of death makes us more attentive to our surroundings because it makes us aware of the *preciousness* of the world. Through coming close to death, we realize that life is temporary, that we will only be able to experience the world for a certain amount of time. As a result, Iris and Carrie have begun to pay more attention to it, in the same way that a person who's moving to a different country really savours the last few days with his family and friends at home. Iris and Carrie – and Cheryl too – have made an unconscious decision to focus on the present rather than to let their attention be immersed in thoughts and daydreams.

3

THE POINT OF
TRANSFORMATION

Another common thread of Cheryl's, Iris's and Carrie's experiences is that they were gradual. They really did experience post-traumatic *growth* in the sense that they went through a gradual process of change, including a process of acceptance and adjustment, after an initial period of depression and frustration. However, in my experience this is quite unusual. Most of the people I spoke to didn't experience a gradual transformation, but a sudden and dramatic one. Their spiritual awakening wasn't incremental; they could pinpoint a *moment* when they experienced a sudden shift, when a powerful and permanent psychological change occurred inside them, after which they felt reborn, with a new perspective and a new relationship to the world.

This is the third and most dramatic type of spiritual alchemy – when suffering leads to sudden and abrupt spiritual awakening.

This shift is always heralded by a powerful awakening experience. The person usually expects the experience to fade after a while, as awakening experiences generally do, but it doesn't. The mould of the normal psyche dissolves away completely, as if it's been blown apart with such force that it isn't able to reform itself. A new kind of psychic structure takes its place and the person has a new identity and a new experience of the world. The awakened state endures and eventually the person realizes that it's now their normal state.

Over the next three chapters we're going to look at how different types of trauma can give rise to this sudden transformation, beginning with stress, upheaval and bereavement. Although these often cause a disintegration of the personality, through a nervous breakdown or a major depressive episode, they can sometimes have the opposite effect and lead to a major *integration*.

'ANOTHER KIND OF LIGHT'

One person who has experienced this very profoundly is an American lady called Jamie Parnam. Jamie is now 67 years old; her transformative experience happened 25 years ago, although in some respects the turmoil that triggered it began much earlier.

Jamie became pregnant with twins at the age of 20. In the 1960s, particularly in the southern United States, it wasn't acceptable to be a single mother, so she married the twins' father. But there was constant stress between them and it soon became clear that they were incompatible. Although she wasn't religious, Jamie felt guilty that she couldn't live happily with her husband, believing that she had disappointed her family. However, she had another child with the man and they stayed together for the sake of the children.

Jamie's husband's job meant that he was away a lot, and eventually, years later, she found out he was having an affair. By this time, her twins were away at college and she decided it was finally time for her and her husband to separate. But as she was planning to go, she learned that her husband's business had gone bankrupt. The IRS took the house, and the bank told her that all their money was gone.

After the separation, Jamie and her younger daughter lived together until her husband stopped paying alimony and child support. Since she didn't have a job, or any other access to money, she couldn't provide for her daughter, who went to live with her husband.

Living alone without any money, Jamie became severely depressed and spent most of her days asleep. When she was awake, she drank and took pills to try to numb her pain. She never tried to kill herself, but felt as though she had given up on life. She often went to sleep hoping that she wouldn't wake up the next morning. She decided that her situation was hopeless and that the only course of action was to accept her lot and expect nothing else. She felt there was nothing she could do to improve her life and so there was no point trying. As a result, she stopped thinking about herself and her problems. And looking back now, she believes that this was the reason why she had a transformational experience, because she had 'surrendered' and stopped being so self-absorbed.

Finally she managed to 'get a little bit of a grip' and took a job at the local governor's office. And just a few days after starting the job, she had what she describes as 'the most wonderful experience of my life':

I was driving home from work one afternoon when
I noticed the sun shining into my car window. It was
quite bright and became very large and I soon realized
it wasn't just the sun but another kind of light.

And that's how things started. The light was intense but not blinding. It seemed to be warm but not hot. It had the essence of being alive and thoughtful, kind and loving. I happened to be on a street lined with big oak trees and, as I was enveloped by this light, I noticed the branches of the trees were in the car with me. Not only were they in my car, but I was in them. I could see the cellular structure of the leaves and I was a part of their movement. I was part of their molecular structure. I thought at the time, 'How odd, but isn't it nice!' Then 'nice' moved on to pure joy and bliss. All of a sudden I felt I knew the secret of everything. I possessed all the knowledge there was and I knew that everything and everybody was all right. I didn't need to worry about anything. The love was palpable. I thought I might explode with joy.

Ultimately, these things receded and I found myself about two blocks or so further down the road. Evidently I had continued to drive my car, but I had no conscious memory of doing so.

I found myself left with a feeling of serenity, love, joy and lack of fear for myself or anyone else.

This is a high-intensity awakening experience, a mystical vision of the oneness and harmony of the universe. And it was also a point of transformation, when Jamie underwent a permanent psychological shift. When the initial experience of joy and meaning faded, she was aware that she was a different person:

From the moment the experience receded into the background, I knew there was nothing to be afraid of.

My brain and body didn't respond with fear. There was a calmness inside me rather than the flight-or-fight sensation. And I still have that sense of fearlessness now.

Material things don't matter to me any more. I'm not interested in buying things or trying to impress other people. Before then, I was very self-conscious and I cared a lot about what people thought of me. But my perspective changed and I realized I was no longer at the centre of things. I realized that there were many other things that were much more important than me. At the same time I think it made people like me a lot more – not that that was my goal. I think I became a more genuine, considerate and caring person and that was very apparent to the people around me. I became less judgemental and more compassionate and tolerant.

I was never particularly religious, but ever since I've been interested in spirituality. I read a lot of Thomas Merton and he led me to Buddhism. Now I look at everything differently. I appreciate everything, even the ugly things.

JANICE'S SPIRITUAL EMERGENCY

A few years ago, when I was doing an MSc in transpersonal psychology, one of my fellow students was a gentle, softly spoken lady called Janice. She had a very calm aura around her, a quality of detachment and self-sufficiency. When I asked her about her interests, she told me that she was a member of the 'spiritual crisis' network, an organization set up by Stan Grof and his wife Christina to support people going through 'spiritual emergencies'.

What Grof calls a 'spiritual emergency' is very similar to the experiences we're looking at in this book: an intense and dramatic experience which disturbs the normal stable structure of the mind, releasing new energies and potentials and so bringing the possibility of psychological transformation. According to Grof, spiritual emergencies can be triggered by meditation, yoga, powerful sexual experiences or extreme physical exertion. Perhaps most commonly, however, they are triggered by a traumatic emotional experience. As Grof writes, 'This can be loss of an important relationship, such as the death of a child or another close relative, divorce, or the end of a love affair. Similarly, a series of failures or the loss of a job or property can immediately precede the onset of spiritual emergency.'[1]

And the reason why Janice was so interested in this subject was, she told me, because she had experienced a powerful spiritual transformation herself.

It had started ten years previously, when her husband suddenly had a stroke. He was paralysed down one side of his body and in hospital for months. He became very depressed and Janice found it difficult to cope looking after him at the same time as working and caring for their children. The stress led to a terrible row with her husband, which ended with her storming out of the hospital. Something inside her snapped and she felt as if she didn't know herself any more, or her husband. She went for a long walk to think things through and it was during this walk that she had a powerful spiritual experience, which I've already quoted in *Waking from Sleep*:

I ran out to Hilbury Island, and I had an amazing experience where I was at one with the seabirds. It was absolutely beautiful and fantastic. There was definitely a feeling of oneness, a really strong feeling of affinity with the birds. The sun was coming down in shafts of light from the clouds and it was just all beautiful.

I walked back from the island and there was an old man walking his dog, and I could really feel the love that he had for his dog and the dog for him. I could feel other people's emotions. There was a runaway horse and I caught him. I held him and was really conscious of how he was anxious and how he calmed down slowly.

Exactly as it was for Jamie, this powerful awakening experience was also Janice's point of transformation. She suddenly felt as if her old life was meaningless and her old self a kind of ghost. This feeling of being a new person was so strong that she felt she had to test herself:

I thought that if I really was a new person I could do something I hadn't been able to do before and decided to try underwater swimming. Before that I hadn't liked getting my face wet, but now I found I could swim a width underwater after just a couple of tries. I felt I had shed some barriers that were holding me back and I could do all sorts of things I couldn't do before. It was wonderfully liberating and exciting. I tried pushing myself to the limit by doing various things.

Janice felt that she had to make changes in her daily life as well, and decided that she was going to leave her husband. This added to the turmoil, especially for her children. They were all finding it difficult to sleep and sometimes stayed up all night together. Janice had several other spiritual experiences, but the euphoria was offset by a sense of confusion. The problem, she realizes now, was that she didn't have any context in which to understand her experience, partly because she had no knowledge of spirituality and psychology: 'I had no idea what had happened and was in a very vulnerable and open state. If this had happened within the context of a recognized spiritual practice with the support of a spiritual community it would have been different, but I was alone with no framework.'

The stress and sleeplessness led to some psychiatric problems. Janice stopped eating, felt freezing cold all the time and began to lose her memory. She was admitted to a psychiatric unit and it took her several weeks to recover. But once she had regained her equilibrium, her new sense of identity persisted. She felt a new sense of the complexity of life, whereas before she had always felt that it was straightforward. She became less materialistic, more sensitive to the beauty of nature and more compassionate towards the sufferings of others. She began to study psychology and to read books about spirituality, which had never interested her at all before. As she summarises her new outlook:

I'm aware of lots of different perspectives, whereas things used to be black and white. I pick up on a lot of things, and when I see that other people don't notice them, I think, 'Should I mention it?' You're always in a different world slightly.

I can feel connections, lots of relatedness, how groups of people work together and create a dynamic that you can feel. Sometimes you get caught up in it, other times you can just sit and observe it.

My relationships are certainly different. I'm more empathic and aware of other people's feelings. For example, a friend of ours has been diagnosed with cancer and everyone else seems to avoid talking about it. But I have this sense that we really have to do what we can for him and go to see him, and quickly.

I appreciate nature more too. I feel more connected to it and realize that I need it. That was the big change, I think, and I have restructured my life to include that. I've had more experiences of connection with animals (horses and seabirds mostly) but none quite as dramatic as that one on the island.

I have the feeling that I need to respect spiritual values and live by them. And I ride horses – for me that's almost a spiritual discipline, that sort of communication with the horse.

I still like nice things, but I'm not as materialistic as I used to be. I have a couple of really nice rings that we inherited from my husband's family. I really used to love wearing these rings and always wore them when we went out. I think I was proud of them because of their value. Well, somehow that doesn't bother me any more and I've gone off them. I still wear them occasionally to please my husband, but I can't really be bothered with them. They just seem like relics now. Part of the reason I liked them was because of their monetary value and that just doesn't seem to fire me up any more.

I'm just more relaxed about things. Before I used to dash around mindlessly doing and buying things without ever really knowing why. I used to really feel that I needed things more and that I'd be deprived if we didn't have a foreign holiday and I'd always be looking at brochures. But now it doesn't bother me.

It feels like a permanent change. You can't go back, you can't undo things, you can't unknow things. My view of the world had been very simplistic. I'd thought things were easy and straightforward – that's how I'd lived my life. I've unlearnt a lot of things.

'THEN THE FLOODGATES OPENED...'

Another example of a state of permanent awakening caused by intense stress and upheaval was given me by an American lady named Stephanie. She went through a long period of turmoil which began when she had a stillborn baby at the age of 25. This led to a long period of sadness and misfortune when 'everything continued to go downhill... Hard to imagine that life could be so difficult, but it was. One mishap after another. Sadness, misunderstandings, betrayals.'

In her mid-forties Stephanie felt as though her misfortune was finally at an end when she fell deeply in love for the first time in her life. For two years she was in a state of blissful happiness, feeling as if she had found her soulmate. But then, completely unexpectedly, her partner ended the relationship. This caused a final crescendo of suffering. Like Jamie, Stephanie felt there was no point striving for anything more in her life. She gave up her master's degree and was 'determined just to work, eat and sleep'. At this time she was working in the operating room of a busy hospital and became very sensitive to the pain and suffering she was witnessing on a daily basis. Finally, six months after the break-up of her relationship, she experienced a spiritual transformation:

Everything just began unravelling. I began doing the oddest life review. I called friends I hadn't seen since high school. I saw patterns of dysfunction that spanned generations within my family. I thought I must be dying, because my whole life was unfolding before me in the most integrated and cohesive way. My messy, insignificant life seemed perfect. It couldn't have been any other way.

Then the floodgates opened, the water broke. It went on for three days. On the third day I was filled with pure light, 'the peace that passeth all understanding'. I entered a state of bliss that lasted several months. I guess I can say I gave birth to myself or to 'the self'. Through it all I stayed grounded, was oriented to time, place, etc., and I was able to work. I did leave my job shortly after, taking several months off to adjust to the change in consciousness. To sum it up as a scientist, I experienced a frequency change. To sum it up in spiritual terms, it was an initiation.

I pretty much live in the present moment now. My mind is clear; when I meditate, it's silent. The most profound change has been the disappearance of egoic consciousness. There's no little voice in the head. I don't have the ego's constant prompting and fixation on regret and fear. Thinking is not something I do very much any more. This is the most remarkable side effect of the transformation – the lack of internal noise ... and judgement. Although I have opinions about what's happening in the world, there's no attachment emotionally. My opinions are more observations of how things appear to be. If I lapse into any sophomoric behaviour, I'm aware of it almost instantly, but there is no internal judgement against myself for having done so, nor are the lapses very serious.

I enjoy doing nothing. I'm rarely, if ever, unhappy. Although I spend a good bit of time alone, I'm never lonely. I enjoy solitude a great deal. I feel whole, and at peace. In many ways I feel that I'm still in a cooling-off period, on ice. When the floodgates of consciousness open, it takes a bit of time to reground.

Relationships have changed in that I'm not invested in them in the traditional ways. I don't worry about them any more. For example, I used to worry about my children, but I don't do that now. I don't worry about anything.

I view love in a completely different way now. Love is a state of grace. It just is. What an amazing gift it is to experience love as a state of being rather than as a conditional 'feeling' that comes and goes.

So far, it would seem, it's a permanent transformation. I wonder from time to time if I'll slip back into the old way of being, but it hasn't happened yet.

BEREAVEMENT: 'THE SHUTTERS WERE BEING PULLED UP ONE BY ONE'

Stephanie's suffering began with the birth of her stillborn daughter, just as, in the last chapter, Carrie's trans-formational journey began with the death of her nephew.

Bereavement is the most severe type of upheaval and loss we can experience. The death of our loved ones – our parents, our spouses, our siblings and children – often leaves a pain so great, and a hole so deep and wide, that it may take decades to heal over, and may never even heal at all. But precisely because it's such an acute kind of suffering, bereavement can be a catalyst for growth or transformation.

Studies have shown that powerful post-traumatic growth can follow from bereavement. The psychologist Stephen Shuchter found that, two years after losing their partners, most widows or widowers felt they had grown as a result of the bereavement. They felt they could see life from a wider perspective, were less affected by trivial worries and more appreciative of important things. They felt that they had become more sensitive, more self-reliant, more open and more spiritual in their everyday lives.[2] While according to another psychologist who has studied bereavement and grief, Dennis Klass, once someone has come to terms with the death of a loved one, 'the person feels his or her life is more authentic, more meaningful'.[3] (In Chapter 6, we'll see that one of the most famous spiritual teachers of the twentieth century, J. Krishnamurti, underwent a spiritual transformation following a series of bereavements.)

Another person whose spiritual transformation began with bereavement is a 54-year-old woman from the north-east of England called Glyn Hood. In 2005, her 21-year-old daughter, Lauren, started to have terrible stomach pains and was told she had appendicitis. She had an operation, which seemed to go smoothly, but three days later she died, for reasons which have never been explained. The hospital couldn't account for it and an inquest didn't provide any answers; eventually the family was told it was probably a case of 'sudden adult death syndrome' or possibly caused by an inherited heart condition.

The death was especially tragic because Lauren had a one-year-old baby. And for Glyn herself, it led to a series of other problems. She had been running a plumbing and heating business with her husband, but they were so devastated that they couldn't function and it closed down almost overnight. Left as a single parent, Glyn's son-in-law had to stop working, which meant Glyn had two families to support. And because there wasn't any clear cause of death, the death certificate was delayed, which meant that Lauren's debts couldn't be written off. Companies she owed money to kept phoning Glyn to demand the money, not accepting that she was dead and adding interest to the payments. In six weeks, a bill for £20 multiplied to hundreds of pounds. Suspecting negligence, Glyn hired medical experts and solicitors to investigate her daughter's death, and within a year she had paid out around £35,000, using up all of her and her husband's savings.

There were other problems too. The elder of Glyn's two young sons, Daniel, was having difficulties at school. He found it hard to communicate or to make friends. Eventually he was diagnosed with Asperger's Syndrome, but only after a long, frustrating process of being given different opinions by counsellors, teachers and psychologists. Her other young son, Bailey, developed a phobia about dying. After his sister's death, he thought he was going to die next and started carrying toy weapons to bed with him. He was frightened of going to sleep because he thought he might not wake up, and had terrible nightmares. 'I'm not frightened of dying,' he told Glyn. 'I'm frightened of the monsters when I get there.'

After so much sadness and stress, Glyn felt as though she was falling apart. She'd always been a strong, resourceful, even arrogant person, and for the first time ever, she felt that she didn't know the answers and that she couldn't cope. She had lost her daughter, her business and all her savings. She felt that Lauren's death was her fault, that if she'd been a good mother she somehow could have prevented it, and that Daniel's personality problems must be her fault too. She also felt guilty for possibly passing on a genetic heart problem to all her children.

'All the structures were breaking down,' she told me. 'I went from being quite egotistical and patronizing to knowing nothing. Everything I had faith in had let me down.'

But at the same time as feeling the strain, Glyn was having occasional 'lightbulb moments', as she calls them. The first one was at Lauren's funeral, when she had a 'knowing that things are not quite as they are. I knew that Lauren wasn't who I thought she was. I knew she couldn't have gone; it was impossible. Her body could die, but she couldn't.'

And finally, two years after her daughter's death, Glyn had an earth-shattering 'lightbulb moment' which signalled a shift to a new identity and to a permanent state of wakefulness. It was just after Daniel had been diagnosed with Asperger's and she had spent the afternoon reading up on the condition. As she describes it:

My mind was blank because I'd been so intensely involved in learning about Asperger's. It was lovely outside, a gorgeous day in early June, with a beautiful blue sky. I had to go to the supermarket and as I was driving into the car park something started to happen. It was as though I had shutters around my brain and they were being pulled up one by one. And knowledge was flooding through. This knowledge was filling me; I was expanding. I had to pull in and just let it happen. I was just sitting there, not knowing what was coming. And it was all coming at once, flooding through, as if my ego was crashing down.

And suddenly I'm aware of everything there is. There's still a physical me, but there's also a real me. I can feel the difference distinctly: the physical me is much heavier; the real me is very light, pure and perfect. Everything's perfect. There's a white spirit in everything, in us, a superior mind, far greater than anything I could have dreamed of. I'm euphoric, joined with God, seeing everything from a much higher perspective.

We're all one. There's just one mind working through each individual body. It's moving through us, creating our thoughts. Everything is connected, inside and outside. I don't need anything because I am everything. I'm one with this great awareness. And I love everything on the planet.

I know that there's nothing bad or wrong. Everything is perfect. It's all how God experiences itself. Everything balances itself; opposites have to be there for it all to work. I know that there is no time. We are eternal; everything happens now. There is no such thing as pain. Oh my God – Lauren couldn't die! I'm absolutely euphoric. She couldn't die because we're part of the same energy. You can't lose anybody because we're all one. Nobody is who they think they are. We're all perfect. There are no disabilities, there are just roles we've been given...

I was so amazed and so euphoric. I watched people scuttling around the car park and thought, 'You have no idea! It's all an illusion, just a dream. I've just been given a glimpse of reality.'

Glyn knew right away that she had changed permanently. Her normal psyche dissolved away completely and has never re-formed. In the three years since the experience, her wakefulness has never faded. I asked her to describe how she had changed and she replied as follows:

The way it feels is that I've permanently broken through to another state. I've moved up to another level of awareness, which I know is going to stay with me. One day, a shift occurs and a different picture suddenly emerges, showing you who you really are – an eternal being, far more powerful and amazing than you ever thought possible. I knew without doubt that I'd witnessed the absolute truth and, having experienced it with such clarity, there's no going back. It's like the transformation a caterpillar goes through during the chrysalis stage before emerging as a butterfly.

I drove my family mad because I was so buzzing with all this. 'You have no idea of who you really are!' I kept telling them. 'It's just a role you're playing and as soon as you realize that, you'll disappear.' At first it presented me with problems: how to remain in this expanded state, which felt like my real home, at the same time as playing the role of mother to a large family, as well as the role I'd established in society. For quite a long time I found myself dipping in and out of situations, feeling a complete fake, an actor playing a part. Eventually I began to cop out altogether, preferring to spend more time alone. Meanwhile I read everything I could, hoping to find other people who'd had the same experience and who could give me advice. I found plenty of theories, but few 'experiencers'.

Now I spend a lot of time in the present. In the past, when friends came round and told me about their problems, I'd get really involved, but now my awareness is somewhere else. When I'm with them, I can feel a white light inside me. I can open my heart and let it flow out. Nothing upsets me the way it used to. Nothing fazes me. I know how to make stressful situations pass by not focusing any emotional energy on them.

Material things don't interest me any more. I used to like home comforts, but now I hate having things I don't need. I feel more inclined to give things away. I have no need for them. Behaviour – our thoughts and deeds – is much more important than material goods. I love being alone – just being still, going inwards. It's ongoing – the deeper I go, the more I realize, and the more I realize, the more amazing it all is.

I also have a strange reluctance to work for a salary now. It feels wrong. If I was going to go back out into the world, it would be where I was asked to do something for somebody. I can't abide the thought of doing a job I wouldn't like and being involved in negative situations. If I'm around people who are negative I instinctively pull away from them. I want to say to them, 'Do you realize what you're putting out into the world?' Because now I know the power of thought.

If people are negative because of their problems, I try to tune into their higher self. Sometimes I can turn it around and introduce them to their higher self. I want to say to them, 'You're a shining light. You have

*this amazing self that you're not aware of.' I can't
see people any other way. I can't dislike anybody.
I'm always sending love back into the world. It's an
electrical flow of love.*

*I have much less of a sense of a separate self. After my
experience, any opinions I'd formed previously about
God/religion or other philosophies became irrelevant –
there's only One and we're joined with it regardless.*

*When I lost my daughter I felt I'd gone to hell and
back, but after glimpsing heaven my grieving ceased
instantly. There is only love; there's no real pain or
suffering or death. It's impossible. My daughter could
never leave me, except in the movie I'd constructed in
my mind, which then played out in the outer world.
Time only exists inside our cocoon; outside of it,
there's eternity. She was always me and I was her.
I am everyone, everyone is me – nothing is
separate.*

QUANTUM CHANGE

All of the shifters we've heard from in this chapter experience
essentially the same state of being as Cheryl, Iris and Carrie
in the last chapter. They have a heightened awareness
and appreciation of beauty and nature and a new sense of
connection to the world. They have become less materialistic
and status-oriented, and are free of anxiety, filled with a sense
that 'all is well'. In other words, they have all experienced
permanent spiritual awakening. In fact, Stephanie and
Glyn both appear to have reached a high level of spiritual
awakening, to the point where their ego-mind has dissolved
away and they no longer feel a sense of separateness.

The only difference is that, again, for these four women this transformation happened suddenly. They didn't transform through a long process of adjustment and development, but through a sudden *leap* – a leap to a higher level of being. It's as if the psychological pressure and tension built up to such intensity – either through a long period of stress and upheaval like Jamie's, or a shorter period of very intense stress like Janice's – that the normal psyche could no longer withstand it and dissolved away. For them, this didn't cause a breakdown but a shift up, to a higher self.

This prompts the question *why* does intense stress and upheaval cause a psychological breakdown in some people (perhaps most), whereas for others it triggers a permanent spiritual awakening? To make sense of this, it's important to understand the difference between psychotic states and higher states of consciousness. With psychological disorders, the normal ego breaks down as a structure. The normal 'self-system' dissolves, so that it can no longer properly perform normal functions like perception, cognition and self-control. The person no longer has a stable sense of identity and may experience perceptual and cognitive distortions, such as when people with schizophrenia see hallucinations or hear voices inside their head. But with higher states of consciousness, the self-system is still intact. There's still a stable sense of self, but it's a different *kind* of self. For these four women, the self-system wasn't destroyed as a structure; instead there was a shift to a *different* structure. Rather than breaking apart, it re-formed itself. Rather than disintegrating, it reacted to the intense stress by *re*integrating itself, at a higher level of consciousness, giving birth to a new self. This doesn't exist separately from its surroundings and isn't disturbed by fear and anxiety.

However, it isn't always just a question of either/or. When a person's normal self dissolves due to turmoil and trauma, there may occasionally be a period of psychological instability before they attain real spiritual transformation, before the new self stabilizes, especially if they don't fully understand what's happened to them. Janice's story is a good example of this. As she points out, she had neither support from the people around her nor a philosophical framework to help her make sense of her experience, and that was part of the reason for her psychological problems.

4

SUDDEN TRANSFORMATION: ILLNESS AND DISABILITY

Serious, life-threatening illnesses are much more than a physical problem; they can have devastating psychological effects too, including severe depression and anxiety. How do you cope with the loss of your health and freedom, and the potential loss of your life, with the possibility that your plans and ambitions will be reduced to nothing? We've already seen how illnesses like cancer or ME can lead to gradual spiritual transformation, or post-traumatic growth. But sometimes the psychological trauma of illness can build up to such a pitch of intensity that sudden transformation can occur.

THE SPIRITUAL HEALER

Last year I was invited to Barcelona for some publicity events for the Spanish translation of one of my books. After I had given a lecture at the University of Barcelona, one of the organizers gave me a lift back into the city centre with a friend of his. I had already noticed his friend during the lecture. There was something very striking about her – as well as being very beautiful, she had an unusual glow in her eyes, a look of powerful serenity. During the journey, I asked her about herself and she told me that she was a spiritual healer. I wasn't surprised – I could almost recognize it in her eyes. But what did surprise me was how she had become a healer. She told me that it was the result of becoming ill with multiple sclerosis five years before.

When she was first told she had MS, Berta was devastated. There was an empty feeling in the pit of her stomach, as if she had vertigo. The thought that she would have to live with the disease for the rest of her life terrified and depressed her. Slowly, however, she began to accept the illness and integrate it into her day-to-day life.

A year after the diagnosis, she began some treatment with a powerful drug called Beta Interferon, which she had to inject herself with every two days. For the first few months the treatment went well and her symptoms diminished. But suddenly she began to feel a resistance to it, without understanding why. One day, just as she was about to inject herself, she had a realization: 'This is not the path, not the way to cure yourself.' Impulsively, she threw away the syringe and medication. She felt as though there was a new kind of certainty inside her, almost a new kind of energy.

Earlier, when her illness had been diagnosed, she had regularly had dizzy spells and giddiness, and had assumed it was just part of the normal symptoms of MS. But after this realization she began to pay more attention to these dizzy spells and became aware of them as energy processes. She began to experiment with them, finding that if she sat on the floor with her back straight and allowed the process to work itself out, the dizziness disappeared. She felt much more relaxed, with a lot more energy. She learned to pay full attention to the process and to give herself up to it completely. If she was at work and felt it beginning, she would say that she felt ill and go home to completely focus on it.

She began to attend workshops on channelling energy through movement and meditation, and started to have ecstatic experiences. The nature of the energy was joyful. Whenever it flowed through her it was as if she was floating on an ocean of bliss. Other people could feel it around her too; they told her that they felt invigorated and alert in her presence, even that they felt free of the physical or psychological problems that been afflicting them. Berta realized that she could use the energy to help others, and so she began her work as a spiritual healer.

Like Cheryl, Berta now sees her illness as a gift, which has given her access to a deep-rooted spiritual source which she had not been fully aware of before. She feels like a different person, so much so that when people ask her about her earlier life it's difficult for her to connect it with who she is now. She has a deep sense of contentment and meaning, and – again like Cheryl – she has learned to trust life rather than strive to make things happen. The symptoms of her MS have been alleviated too:

I feel infinitely more content and at peace. I have found a joy that I never experienced even as a child, and, little by little, it's becoming a permanent part of me. I am much more present and happy to be on this planet. I live one day at a time, aware that my life is a mystery, revealing itself as it unfolds.

I've also become much more patient. Before I found it difficult to wait for things to happen, but now I enjoy the waiting. In fact it doesn't bother me much whether things happen or not. I would say that this patience and acceptance are the most profound parts of my transformation.

As a child I was obsessed with the idea of God. I always wondered why I couldn't believe in him while others could. It was a very strange and disturbing feeling; instead of feeling the presence of God, I just felt his absence keenly. But now I feel connected to the God that is within me and the only thing that matters to me is knowing myself and accepting myself just as I am. That is my goal in life.

DISABILITY

How do you think you would feel if you were in an accident and lost the use of all of your limbs? Like illness, disability is much more than a physical problem – along with the loss of the use of parts of their body, a person who becomes disabled has to deal with the loss of their independence and sense of status, the loss of activities they enjoyed and a changed body image. There's no doubt that this can be a traumatic and depressing experience. Nevertheless, there is evidence that the horror you might feel at the prospect of becoming disabled – and the pity you might feel for those who are – is misplaced.

One of the most interesting developments in psychology over recent years has been the positive psychology movement, led by psychologists such as Martin Seligman and Mihaly Csikszentmihalyi. Positive psychologists examine the sources of human happiness and how different activities and experiences affect our level of well-being. They have made some very interesting discoveries: for example, that extremely rich people are not significantly happier than other people, and that after a few months, lottery winners aren't significantly happier than they were before.[1]

Research has also shown that people who become seriously disabled are much happier than we might think. One study found that people who had become paraplegic – that is, who had lost the use of their legs – as a result of spinal cord accidents quickly adapted to their new predicament. After eight weeks they generally reported feeling more positive than negative emotions and after a few years they were only 5 per cent less happy than able-bodied people.[2]

A study of people who had become quadriplegic – that is, paralysed from the neck down – showed similar results. Three months after their accident, they were on average only 10 per cent less happy than before. After a year, they had almost returned to the same level of happiness as before their accident. Eighty-four per cent of people with extreme quadriplegia rated their lives as being 'above average' in quality.[3]

This suggests that becoming disabled is certainly no barrier to happiness. But even more than this, it can be the trigger for permanent awakening.

DR GILL HICKS, MBE: SURVIVOR OF THE 7/7 TUBE BOMBINGS

On the morning of 7 July 2005, three bombs exploded on the London Underground. They were detonated by suicide bombers within 50 seconds of each other, with another exploding on a bus about an hour later. Fifty-six people were killed and around 700 injured.

The most serious explosion on the Underground was the third, on a train pulling out of King's Cross station. Because it happened at a point where the underground tunnel was very narrow, the explosion was more concentrated, and 26 people died on this train alone. One person who was seriously injured in the blast was a young Australian woman named Gill Hicks, who was standing just a few feet away from the suicide bomber.

Gill had been living in London for 13 years, since her early twenties, working in architecture and design. Over the previous couple of years she had been feverishly busy; she was always the first to arrive at her office in the morning and the last to leave in the evening, and most of her mealtimes doubled as meetings. Her career was her life and recently she had started to achieve the success she'd been striving for. After running her own successful publishing company, she had been offered a job as a curator for the Design Council and been made a fellow of the Royal Society of Arts.

Gill was the last person to be pulled alive from the wreckage of the train. In the minutes after the bomb went off, she hovered on the brink of death. She felt herself falling into blackness and experienced the 'life review' common to near-death experiences. As she describes it: 'My life was flashing before my eyes, flickering through every scene, every happy and sad moment, everything I had ever done, said, experienced. It was all being played like a film running at high speed in my head.'[4]

The falling stopped and she was sure she was dead, but then became aware of voices screaming and other faint voices shouting reassurance: 'Stay calm. It's OK.' She couldn't speak and realized that she couldn't feel her legs. Although the carriage was filled with thick grey smoke, she looked down and could see that her legs looked like an anatomical drawing. But rather than panicking, a deep calm arose inside her. She knew that she had to stay calm to survive. If she panicked or screamed, she would lose even more blood. She wanted to close her eyes and sleep, but forced herself to stay awake, hoping that someone would rescue her. There were two voices in her head, one willing her to hold on and survive, the other willing her to let go and allow herself to die. The second voice was beautiful and alluring. She had no fear of death at all – in fact, she longed for the peace it would bring. But she thought about all the people who mattered to her, all the people who loved her, and realized that she had to stay alive for their sake, to spare them the pain of bereavement. And as she made that decision, a rush of energy filled her and the second voice stopped, leaving only her urge to survive.

Then she was aware of a light – torchlight coming towards her. She heard the words 'Priority one' and felt someone placing a tag on her. Feeling that she was in safe hands, she let herself slip into unconsciousness.

Gill's injuries were so severe that both her legs had to be amputated and doctors doubted that she would survive. But after two weeks of intensive care, she began to regain her strength. And as she realized that she was going to survive, she also became aware that she was a different person, who would be living what she referred to as 'Life Two'.

Ever since then, Gill has had a new appreciation of life, an ability to value aspects that she took for granted before:

From the moment I was given the option of choosing life, I made a vow: that if I survived I would live a full life, a good and rich life. I vowed that I would never take anything – all that I have – for granted again. I would never forget how precious every single day is.

I have stayed true to that promise... Once you adopt that attitude and apply it to all areas of life, everything starts to look different... I still make a point of delighting in every mouthful of water, relishing every

drop of coffee or tea, savouring every morsel of food
and taking pleasure in every glass of wine.[5]

This isn't to say that Gill is completely free of regrets. She still misses her legs – not just because of what they enabled her to do, but as a part of her body that she used to have a relationship with. She still daydreams about how great it would be to jump out of bed, to paddle in the sea, to wear jeans and shoes again or to paint her toenails. But at the same time she has a new appreciation of her body, of the miracle of its healing processes and the amazingly intricate and complex things it does every second to keep her healthy and alive. As she watched it heal, it was, she says, 'like witnessing a thousand miracles each and every day. I was in awe of my body; I was in awe of the human spirit.'[6] She felt so grateful to her body that she promised herself she would never do anything to harm it ever again: 'I made a promise, a vow, that I would look after myself, love myself, every day. I would feed my body good food... I wanted to repay it for not letting me down, for continuing the fight, not just for life itself, but for quality of life.'[7]

One positive aspect of losing her limbs, she says, is that she has been forced to live much more slowly, which has given her a heightened awareness of her experience and her surroundings: 'Being slow – physically moving at a slower pace – has been an extraordinary experience. I have seen so much more, just by being able to stop, look and absorb.'[8]

Eight months after the bombings, Gill felt strong enough to return to work. However, her new outlook on life meant that her previous work at the Design Council no longer seemed as important. When she went back to her office to see her colleagues she picked up the 'Urgent' file on her desk, looked through all her reports and records, and threw them all straight in the bin. She soon resigned her position and was invited to become an ambassador for the charity Peace

Direct, and later became an advocate for Leonard Cheshire Disability too. She has recently founded MAD for Peace (Making a Difference for Peace; *see Further Information section for details*), which communicates through innovative and engaging projects everyone's individual responsibility to create a world without extreme conflict. In 2009 she was awarded an MBE for her services to charity; in the same year, she was also voted Australian of the Year in the UK and awarded an honorary doctorate in philosophy for her contribution to the worlds of design and charity. For her, 'Life Two' has been an awakening, an invigorating and massively meaningful journey.

MICHAEL HUTCHISON

One person who has overcome even more severe difficulties than Gill Hicks, and been transformed even more radically and positively, is the American writer Michael Hutchison. Michael has suffered the most serious disabilities a human being can possibly suffer, without becoming self-pitying or despondent. In fact, he has become as happy and fulfilled as it is possible to be.

In 1998, Michael was a successful author in the field of science and spirituality. His book *Megabrain*, on how brain technology can be used to induce higher states of consciousness, had been a bestseller, and he had recently published another successful book about his experiments with flotation tanks. He regularly travelled across America and Europe, giving lectures and doing workshops, and had a young son he adored, who lived half the time with him and half with his ex-wife. He had recently started a new book which was going very well and had every reason to look forward to the future.

But then two tragic events occurred. The first was a fire. As Michael describes it:

One night I woke up, and the house was filled with black smoke. I ran out of my bedroom and saw my office was on fire, at the other end of the house, and I went running up there to put out the fire, but when I opened the door, I got hit by a wall of black smoke, which suffocated me and knocked me out. I almost died of smoke inhalation, but the worst thing was that almost everything I owned burned up, including the new book I was working on, all my notes, all my research, all my past writings on the computer and the manuscripts. It's a big blow as a writer to see your entire life go up like that.

This was serious enough, but the second event was much more tragic. Michael was a keen runner; he loved running as a way of making himself feel mentally alert and generating new ideas for writing. But one day, shortly after he left hospital, he slipped and had a serious fall while running. Since he is such an articulate and fluent writer and speaker, from this point I'll let him tell his story in his own words. I've put together the following account from my own conversations with him and his own written account of his experience, which he was kind enough to send me:

I got caught in a snowstorm and was heading for home, and I slipped on an ice patch on a bridge and fell head over heels a long distance down, onto the riverbed. My neck and the back of my head smashed into the rocks. Basically, I was lucky I didn't get killed in the fall. I broke my spine. I was lying there in the icy waters, paralysed from the neck down, with only my face out of the water. I knew I was paralysed, and I couldn't call for help, because I couldn't breathe. And the frustrating thing was, I knew I was freezing to death, because I could feel the icy water just sucking the heat out of me.

Over a period of time I just felt myself dying. In fact I did die, as far as I know. It was an interesting experience. I felt as if I was just floating away down the river, and I let go. It was very peaceful. That was the first time I felt a sense of total bliss and the feeling of being home at last. Totally welcome, my place. There was no sense of other people, or of me as a person. The person that had been me was dead. There was a sense of a cosmic consciousness. Totally comfortable. In bliss. It went away when I woke up. I wanted to stay.

Anyway, I woke up in the operating room, having neurosurgery done on my spinal cord. I smashed five cervical vertebrae and almost died of head trauma from the fall, hypothermia and again from my spinal cord injury. The next time I woke up, I was in the intensive care unit again, dying from pneumonia. So, what I was dealing with was a number of near-death experiences in a short period of time. It knocked the wind out of me. I was feeling very low and very tired. I was paralysed from the neck down and, to make it worse, I had to wear a whole body brace that kept me totally stiff, up to the back of my head, with the tip of my chin pointing way up in the air, to keep me from moving my neck, so that the vertebrae, which had been fused in the operation, could heal.

Aside from the pain of the injuries, being unable to move was true misery – trapped in a painful position, without being able to move at all. I spent months totally paralysed with the brace on. I couldn't do anything but stare directly at the ceiling, so my entire visual field was blank, and at first it was so incredibly mind-numbing you can't possibly imagine it. I couldn't read – which was the most agonizing loss to me, since I usually read several books every day – couldn't watch movies, watch people, use the phone or the computer, or have a conversation or have sex.

To make it even worse, the doctors told me I could expect to be a quadriplegic for the rest of my life. They didn't offer any hope of regaining much movement. I thought, 'To hell with that,' and spent hours and hours, for months, trying to get movement in my arms and legs.

After I'd been in the hospital for about four months, my money ran out. Medicaid wouldn't cover me any more. So I had to leave, and there was no place for me to go. I was still pretty much paralysed, although I was getting some movement back in my arms and legs. My only course of action was to get admitted to a very grim nursing home where old people were wandering around shouting, screaming and yelling for help. The screaming never let up. It was like hell. The first year I was there, I truly bottomed out. I felt depressed and I couldn't seem to think very clearly. I wished I didn't have to wake up and I was in constant pain.

I started thinking my life was over. I remember thinking, 'I still feel young, but I can't move. I'm a writer, but I can't move my hands, and I can't write. I'm a thinker, but I can't think clearly.' I had to face it. This was real life. Everything was over. The book

I was working on had disappeared and would never reappear. I had ended a long-term relationship a couple of months before the fire, so I didn't have any companionship that I could fall back on or count on. I was totally alone and thought I would never have a relationship again. Things seemed pretty bleak.

After months of frustration, it began to hit me. The voice in my head said, 'Let go, man, let go. Look at how you're holding on. What do you think life's telling you? All these near-death experiences – what do you think that's all about? Dying, that's what. You keep hanging onto life like you're afraid to let go. It's time to die.' I realized my ego was holding on, trying to keep control. I knew it was time to let go.

Just at this point, they came to take me for a shower. They wheeled me down the hallway and hosed me off and as they wheeled me back to my room I suddenly found things began to happen. It was as if my entire being had been clenched in a tight fist and suddenly the fist opened up and let go completely. Everything dropped away. I began seeing and experiencing a kind of upwelling or emanation inside me. It was in front of my eyes, but also inside my eyes and inside my body, and it started flowing upward. It was emptiness, the void, but it was luminous. It was just a current of bliss. Over the next few hours, it became more and more intense.

As the days went by, I began to realize that I was existing in a sea of bliss. The simple beingness of being was bliss. It was fun to be alive. Every moment, even though I was in a lot of pain and was paralysed, there was still an intrinsic joy at being alive. I began to feel this bliss all around me.

I experimented with going into the bliss and each time I found it easier. I found that there was such an infinite amount to know that I didn't think I could ever understand it. I spent several months just staring at my ceiling and going deeper and deeper inside myself. I learned to slip into blissful nothingness as a way of managing the pain. I disappeared and the pain was left behind. When the spiritual teacher Ramana Maharshi was dying of cancer, people would come to him and say, 'You must be in so much pain.' And he would smile and say, 'Yes, madam, there is pain, but there is no suffering.' That's how it was for me.

It's now 13 years since Michael's accident and he's still in a state of bliss. His pain is still very intense – the soft padding between his lumbar vertebrae has disappeared due to chronic degenerative arthritis, so that his bones grind together whenever he moves his back. Even sitting up is very painful. But what he calls 'going into nothingness' is so effective as pain relief that he has even refused his doctor's offer of inserting a permanent morphine drip into his spine.

As well as an intense feeling of bliss, Michael has an awareness that the whole world – the whole universe even – is pervaded with spiritual radiance. This radiance pervades everything and everyone, so that everything has essentially the same nature and is essentially one.

I feel oneness all the time – I can feel it with you now. It's there from the moment I wake up. How can there be more than one? As I say, I first felt this radiant bliss like a vibration all over inside myself. But the more I got into it, the more I realized that it extended everywhere and connected everything together – all of the planets, all of the cosmos, everything in the universe.

It's an invisible radiance. Every cell in your body generates light, a light that's only visible to the inner eye. You have to have this awakening experience before it becomes visible. The light is the radiance, you can't separate it. It's radiant light bliss. The important thing is to let yourself be conscious and aware. No thoughts, no ideas, no images, nothing. That's what it all comes down to, to be nothing. I learned to be nothing. And that's the bliss.

Because of this sense of oneness, Michael has a heightened sense of compassion. Compassion is more than just the ability to imagine ourselves in other people's shoes, it's an experience of *connection*, of our shared identity. When we feel compassion, we directly sense the sufferings of others through the consciousness that we share with them. That's why compassion increases as we become less selfish and egocentric – because the ego 'walls us off' from other people, breaks us off into islands of individuality. Michael doesn't appear to experience any ego-separateness any more, and so senses this shared identity very strongly. As he says, 'People can sense that I feel one with them. They can sense my compassion, and as a result my relationships are much better than they were before.'

Michael has lost all fear of death and has a constant freshness of perception and a sense of the miraculous nature of life:

Once you know that the bliss of life continues and is amplified in the bliss of death, you will have no fear of death any more. For most people the fear of death, even though they don't think of it, is always there, lurking in their subconscious mind. Once you've lost your fear of death, your life changes in virtually every way. Fear and anxiety no longer exist in your life.

I have realized that just plain life itself is a pure miracle in every second! I can never get enough of it. Everywhere I look things that previously were just ordinary parts of life seem to have a special aura. Everything I look at has this beautiful and uncanny clarity. It's just a pure pleasure to be in the world.

It's a miracle that I'm alive at all, but when you live with the constant experience of being lived through by Consciousness, you see that everything is a miracle, every instant, pain or pleasure, good or bad. It's all a miracle, emerging out of emptiness – that is, consciousness – instant by instant.

I love doing nothing. In the summer I can just sit in a reclining chair on my front porch and watch the leaves on the trees, the birds, an ant crawling up my leg. I just disappear.

One of the most common characteristics of the shifters' new state of being is an awareness that there's no need to strive, to force events to happen. This is the patience that Berta described earlier. There's a willingness to let events unfold as they will and a sense that if we do this, all will be well. Michael feels this very strongly:

When I truly understood this, it was liberating to me, and it took a huge weight off my shoulders. I was

totally free. Everything I did was God's will... I breathed
freely and easily and deeply and effortlessly. Everything
happened effortlessly. And that freedom was Pure
Being – the freedom to do good and the freedom to do
evil, and the freedom to do all the stuff that's between
good and evil.

Like Gill Hicks, Michael isn't completely free of regret – he misses being able to run, for example. But as he told me, 'What the hell, I'm in bliss! Why would anybody give up what I have? Looking back, I thought I was a really happy man, but now it's even better.'

Could there be any story more inspiring than Michael's? All of the stories in this book illustrate the amazing resources of the human spirit, but his shows this more than any other. It's surely tremendously reassuring to learn that a human being can transcend the kind of massive tragedy he suffered, not just in terms of learning to *cope* with it, but in terms of gaining access to a state of intense peace and joy. His story shows that no matter how much turmoil and misery we go through, it can't destroy us. Even at the point of deepest desolation, there's still the potential for recovery and transcendence. In fact there is *much more* potential for transcendence at this point than when life is easy and going according to plan.

One reason why Michael's story is so remarkable is because he has made the biggest leap – the leap from the deepest level of tragedy to the highest intensity of awakening. As I suggested in *Waking from Sleep*, there are different intensities of awakening, both for temporary spiritual experiences and for wakefulness as a permanent state. At a lower intensity of awakening, the world becomes more real and alive and an atmosphere of harmony seems to pervade it. As awakening intensifies, we realize that the source of this harmony is a radiant energy which pervades everything, a kind of underlying ocean of spirit (*Brahman*, as the Indian Upanishads call it). We feel uplifted inside, filled with a sense that 'all is well' and the universe is benevolent and meaningful. Then, at a slightly higher intensity, we can sense the oneness of everything – we realize that, with this spirit-force pervading the world, there is no separation. Everything is a part of everything else and has the same source. And we experience ourselves as part of this oneness too; we realize that, in a sense, we *are* everything around us. And then, at what is perhaps the highest intensity of awakening – absolute wakefulness, as I call it – the whole material world dissolves away, leaving an ocean of pure spirit, and we become part of the blazing, radiant ground of reality.

Most of the shifters we've heard so far have described characteristics of a lower- to medium-intensity wakefulness – a heightened sense of awareness, a sense of meaning and inner well-being and connection to the world. But Michael's wakefulness is of a higher intensity – perhaps even higher than Stephanie's or Glyn's – to the point where he can always see *Brahman* pervading all things, giving them radiance and bringing them into unity, where he can continually sense his own oneness with all things and where he is aware of them arising from the 'emptiness' of pure consciousness, the 'ground' of reality. He has clearly reached the high intensity of wakefulness which, throughout history, has been referred to as enlightenment.

5

SUDDEN TRANSFORMATION: **ADDICTION AND DESOLATION**

Most of the experiences we've looked at so far have been related to *loss*. Trauma and turmoil are often caused by the loss of something central to our lives, something we depend on for our well-being. For Cheryl, this was the loss of independence and status. For Iris and Carrie, this was the loss of their health and the potential loss of their life. For Jamie it was the loss of her family and her house, while for Stephanie it was initially the loss of her baby and finally, many years later, the loss of her partner. For Berta, Gill and Michael, it was the loss of their health and freedom, of the use of parts of their body, and the potential loss of their life.

Loss is like damage to a building – it opens us up, breaks us into pieces and may take us close to the point of complete collapse. The 'building' that suffers this damage is, of course, the ego. But at the same time, as we have seen, this offers the opportunity for a new self to emerge, like a phoenix from the ashes. When the normal ego is damaged or dismantled, a new kind of structure can form in its place, creating a new identity with a new vision of and relationship to the world.

One area where the effects of loss – both destructive and transformative – are very visible is addiction. Alcoholics and drug addicts often move through a slow and painful process of intensifying loss. As their addiction becomes more and more severe, their lives gradually fall apart. Typically, they lose their family, their friends, their career, their house, their money, their hopes and their self-respect, until they reach the point of complete destitution, when they are reduced to nothing and hit rock bottom. Some addicts never recover – they might commit suicide or die from ill-health. But there's at least a chance that, at this point of desolation, they may undergo spiritual transformation.

BILL WILSON

The possibility of spiritual transformation is at the heart of the philosophy of Alcoholics Anonymous. AA's 12-step programme can be interpreted as a path of spiritual development, with some similarities to the eightfold path of Buddhism. The first three steps encourage the alcoholic to recognize the spiritual nature of their problem, recognizing that only 'a power greater than ourselves could restore us to sanity'. This is followed by the decision to 'to turn our will and our lives over to the care of God as we understand Him'. After this, the steps describe a process of rigorous self-examination, as the person recognizes their faults and the harm they have done to others. These steps are partly aimed at making a person less self-centred, to increase the possibility of transformation. Then the person practises prayer and meditation to 'improve our conscious contact with God as we understand Him'. Then finally, 'having had a spiritual awakening as the result of these steps', they are encouraged to spread this message to other alcoholics and help them to become free of their addiction.[1]

This spiritual emphasis isn't surprising, bearing in mind that one of the co-founders of Alcoholics Anonymous, Bill Wilson, experienced spiritual transformation himself.

It's possible to trace Bill Wilson's alcoholism back to a tragedy he suffered at the age of 17, when the girl he intended to marry died. This depressed him so much that he couldn't graduate from high school. He started drinking heavily soon after and was already an alcoholic by his early twenties. After the First World War, he studied law, but never graduated because he was too drunk to pick up his diploma. He began to work as a financial speculator and had some success, until he turned up drunk to too many meetings and business associates began to avoid him.

By his early thirties, Wilson was drinking two – and sometimes three – bottles of cheap gin a day. Every morning he woke up shaking violently and needed a tumbler of gin and several bottles of beer before he was ready to eat his breakfast. Due to his ruined reputation and the Wall Street Crash of 1929, work was hard to find. Occasionally a deal would earn him a few hundred dollars, which would end up in the tills of local bars. When all else failed, he stole money from his wife's purse to feed his addiction.

It wasn't that he didn't want to stop drinking – he tried many times, but no matter how great his resolve, he always relapsed. There were times when he thought he'd beaten his addiction, but then someone would offer him a drink and the next thing he knew he'd be waking up a day later after a binge, unable to remember what had happened. Once, after several days without drinking, he went into a café to use a telephone and the next moment – almost unconsciously – he was at the bar ordering a whisky.

Wilson relapsed so many times that he began to lose hope. He started to think he was insane and was filled with a constant sense of anxiety, a feeling that something terrible was about to happen. He hardly ever ate and was 40 pounds (two and a half stone) under his natural weight. He thought about killing himself, but suppressed his self-hatred by drinking even more. But eventually the desire to commit suicide became uncontrollable. As he described it: 'Then came the night when the physical and mental torture was so hellish I feared I would burst through my window, sash and all. Somehow I managed to drag my mattress to a lower floor, lest I suddenly leap. A doctor came with a heavy sedative.'[2]

The next day he mixed the sedative with gin and became delirious. He was taken to Towns hospital in New York, which specialized in treating alcoholics. At the time most people saw alcoholism as a moral failing, the result of self-indulgence and a lack of self-control, but Towns hospital took the progressive view (for the time) that it was an illness, with both physical and mental symptoms.

Viewing his condition in these terms gave Wilson self-knowledge and courage, and after a regime of exercise and hydrotherapy, he felt that he was finally ready to stop drinking for good. He was dry for four months, but eventually relapsed again. And this time he was sure it was the end. As he put it, 'The curve of my declining moral and bodily health fell off like a ski-jump... This was the finish, the curtain, it seemed to me.'[3]

He went back to Towns hospital, where even the doctors gave up on him. They told his wife that he would be dead within a year at the most, either of heart failure during delirium tremens or of a 'wet brain' (Wernicke-Korsakoff syndrome, caused by vitamin deficiency due to malnutrition).

As he wrote, 'No words can tell of the loneliness and despair I found in that bitter morass of self-pity. Quicksand stretched around me in all directions. I had met my match. I had been overwhelmed. Alcohol was my master.'[4]

He started drinking almost as soon as he left the hospital, but then had a visit from an old drinking partner who had stopped drinking after a religious conversion. The friend encouraged Wilson to join the evangelical group that had helped him, but he was sceptical about religion. He'd never been able to accept the notion of a personal God. Then his friend suggested, 'Why don't you choose your own conception of God?' This gave him something to hold on to – he could accept the idea of God as an impersonal universal spirit or higher power and intelligence, one that wasn't attached to the dogma of any religion.

Nevertheless, Wilson carried on drinking, and was admitted to Towns again, mentally and physically broken and close to both insanity and death. But his acceptance of the idea of a higher power had brought about an inner change and opened him to the possibility of transformation. One night at the hospital, he was in bed, writhing in pain and torment, crying out, 'I'll do anything! Anything at all! If there be a God, let him show himself!' At that moment he had an intense awakening experience which signalled a permanent psychological shift:

> *Suddenly, my room blazed with an indescribably white light. I was seized with an ecstasy beyond description... A wind, not of air, but of spirit [blew through me]. In great clean strength it blew right through me. Then came the blazing thought, 'You are a free man.' ...A great peace stole over me and ... I became acutely conscious of a presence which seemed like a veritable sea of living spirit. I lay on the shores of a new world.*[5]

This experience left him with a feeling of serenity and confidence. He felt 'lifted up, as though the great clean wind of a mountain top blew through and through'. He felt reborn and never drank again for the rest of his life. And shortly afterwards, with the help of another alcoholic named Bob Smith, he began to formulate the philosophy of Alcoholics Anonymous, based on the spiritual transformation he'd undergone.

HANDING IT OVER

One person who has benefited greatly from Bill Wilson's work – and who had a similar transformative experience to him – is a friend of mine called Kevin Hinchcliffe. Kevin was a counselling tutor at a college where I used to teach. I saw him around a few times and felt instinctively that he was someone I should talk to. In an environment where most people were stressed and irritable, his cheerfulness and relaxed manner stood out. There was a light in his eyes which seemed to come from a place of deep contentment inside him.

Not long afterwards, I went to the counselling staff-room to enquire about a student and fell into conversation with Kevin. We found out straightaway that we had a lot in common: we were both interested in transpersonal psychology and had even studied the subject on the same master's degree (in different years). He told me that he meditated too, and was a qualified hypnotherapist. As well as teaching at our college, he worked at a hospital, as a therapist and counsellor for cancer patients.

Soon afterwards, when I began to spend more time with him, I discovered the source of Kevin's serenity and also the reason why he had become interested in spirituality and begun to work in therapy and counselling.

Several years before, Kevin had been a successful architect. He had his own company, with 18 employees. He lived in a large house in a nice area and bought himself a new car every year. His only problem – not that he would have called it a problem at the time – was that he was an alcoholic. He'd been drinking heavily since his teenage years and was now drinking throughout the day and under the influence of alcohol almost all the time. He was still able to function because, as head of his own company, he could delegate rather than actually do the work himself. And since his job involved travelling around the country a lot, visiting different buildings and sites, other people weren't with him regularly enough to realize the extent of his drinking. He loved the culture of drinking, the camaraderie of his drinking partners and the companionship of fellow drinkers at hotel bars. Occasionally he tried to control his drinking – he would have loved to be just a social drinker, like other people – but was never able to.

Once, in Dubai, he was sitting at a bar and saw a man crying, with a pint of lager in front of him. That the man could be crying and drinking at the same time seemed a bizarre juxtaposition.

'What's the matter?' he asked him.

'I'm an alcoholic,' the man replied. 'I stopped drinking three months ago and I've just started again now. This is my first drink for three months.'

As Kevin says now, 'The idea that this man could have a problem with drinking was a complete puzzle to me. I didn't understand why he would want to stop in the first place.'

But soon afterwards, Kevin's world fell apart. His business collapsed in the recession of the early 1990s, when banks refused to lend money to the construction firms he worked with. An old friend offered him three months' work in Dubai and he came home to find that his wife had left him, taking their children. The house had been repossessed, sold by the bank for half its value. He was £60,000 in debt, with only £2,000 left from his work in Dubai. I'll let him tell this part of the story in his own words:

All my possessions were in a plastic bag, a bin liner – that's all I had. Everything else had gone. And I soon got rid of the £2,000. I bought a car for £200 and drank the rest. I was completely alone and was considering suicide. It seemed like a good option, because there was no light at the end of the tunnel. I knew that my drinking was the real reason why everything had fallen apart and my wife had left. But I'd tried to control it before and it had never worked, so I couldn't see any way out.

But then a thought came to me. My father was a Spiritualist healer and I'd been brought up to believe in life after death. So I knew that death wouldn't solve anything. I had the idea that if I died I'd meet someone, a dead relative or friend, and they'd say to me, 'You've made a complete mess of that, haven't you?'

That really shook me, that thought that death wasn't the end and I would have to go through all of this crap again, so I decided to go to Alcoholics Anonymous. I immediately rang them up and they said there was a meeting around the corner that evening. I went to a meeting every night for three weeks and at the end of that time not only had I stopped drinking, I didn't want to drink.

Somebody suggested that since I had a problem that was too big for me to deal with, I should think about handing it over. I asked, 'Hand it over to who?' They said, 'Well, whatever your higher power is, if you believe that there is some entity out there. Why don't you simply ask them to do it for you?'

So I did it. I actually physically sat down that night and handed it over. I went through the process and said, 'OK, I can't do it by myself, but if you're a higher power, this is within your ability.' So I did and it went. And I would class it as a miracle. Sitting in front of a gas fire in a small room with the wallpaper peeling off, on a chair with horsehair sticking out, I felt so content, so at peace. It was quite unbelievable.

After that, I felt like I was on honeymoon. I didn't have a trouble in the world. I owned nothing; I was happy to own nothing. I looked at other people and felt sorry for them because they didn't have what I had. It's an understanding that there's something working on a higher level than us. It's knowing that we don't have anything to worry about. We try to organize our lives, try to achieve goals and ambitions, but if we're part of something greater, it's predestined. We shouldn't be trying to direct it, we should be following it. It's knowing that we're part of something wonderful and mysterious. The challenge will always be to understand it – but we'll never be able to, because of how insignificant we are compared to whatever that power might be.

It really was an awakening. It's as if there are two people: there's a before and an after. I remember in the depths of my drinking, lying down on a couch and thinking, 'Wouldn't it be beautiful to smell the

*grass again and enjoy it?' Simple things like that were
beyond me. But now things like that are really powerful
for me, smelling newly cut grass in the spring or
looking at a beautiful blue sky in the summer.*

*Since then I've never been unhappy. Discontent is
caused by not having what you think you want. It's
not what you need; it's what you think you want.
If you believe that where you are now is only part
of something far larger, it's very comforting and
empowering and makes you feel very safe.*

*The philosophy I carry with me is that every day little
miracles happen. They've been happening every day
since I handed over, and if I allow them to, they'll keep
happening, as long as I let go and don't own anything
or put my trust in material things.*

*If I could give what's happened to me to everyone else,
it would be wonderful.*

After his awakening, Kevin changed his life completely. He
began to contribute to meetings at Alcoholics Anonymous,
then trained as a counsellor and later as a hypnotherapist,
whilst taking occasional work as an architect. He also studied
anxiety and stress management, and eventually took a part-
time job with cancer patients. For six years, he didn't have a
bank account of his own and had very little money, but being
successful or wealthy no longer mattered to him. Now he
just wanted to help people, to try to bring about in others
the change he'd experienced. He no longer worried about
the future, about finding work or having enough money
to live off. In fact he still never worries about anything. As
he told me, 'I've been working on a shoestring for years,

but something always crops up. If I need some money, it just comes. I know it's going to, so I don't worry about it. People ask me, "Why don't you worry about what's going to happen?" I just tell them it will sort itself out.'

Kevin feels that 'the higher power' that he made contact with when he hit rock bottom 16 years ago has guided him through his new life as a therapist. He hasn't had a drunk since that night and has never even had the desire to drink. As he says, 'People who knew me before say, "It's like you're a different person – we knew you as a drinker with a big flash car." I used to have a new Audi every year. Now I've still got an Audi, but it's 15 years old. It's got 160,000 miles on the clock, but it gets me round. Everyone around me has noticed the difference. It's just taken a long time for them to learn to trust me again.'

It's very significant that this change happened at the point when Kevin 'handed over' his problem. Many of the people we've heard from have described a similar point when they 'let go' or accepted their predicament. For Jamie, this was when she accepted that her situation was hopeless and there was nothing she could do to improve it. For Stephanie, this appears to have been when she 'gave up', while for Michael, it was when a voice inside his head told him to 'let go'. In all cases, it was precisely at this moment of 'letting go' that the transformation occurred. This was when Kevin's 'miracle' occurred, when Michael felt that 'everything dropped away' and when for Stephanie, 'the floodgates opened'. This acceptance allowed the psychological shift to take place, like the release of a valve when pressure has built up to a high point.

The concept of 'handing it over' is at the core of the Alcoholics Anonymous rehabilitation process. The AA approach is holistic – recovery has to happen on a physical, psychological and spiritual level. If a person is to become truly free of alcohol, they have to undergo a spiritual transformation. The self that is addicted to alcohol has to die to enable a new self to emerge. And acceptance and letting go are essential parts of this process.

THE GREATEST MIRACLE IN THE WORLD

This is illustrated by the story of a 56-year-old man named Bob Slater, an ex-National Guardsman from Kansas, and also a recovering alcoholic. Bob believes that he was born an alcoholic. Once, as a toddler, he was at a relative's wedding where there were two bowls of punch, one alcoholic and the other non-alcoholic. He drank from the alcoholic bowl by mistake and immediately loved the feeling of intoxication. After that, whenever his parents had a party, he hung around and drank from people's beer glasses when they weren't looking. During his teens and twenties, he experimented with other drugs, including LSD, heroin and cocaine, but alcohol was always his first choice.

By his late twenties, Bob was drinking a bottle of bourbon a day, and his life was falling to pieces. He had trained as a builder and started his own construction business remodelling houses, but spent so much time and money drinking that he neglected his work, and the business failed. At one point he bought a bar, but that failed too, after he was arrested for drink-driving. He was given a DUI – Driving Under the Influence – which under Kansas law meant he wasn't allowed to own a bar or club that sold alcoholic drinks. He was forced to sell the bar at a loss.

All through his years of drinking, Bob was in psychological turmoil. As he told me, 'I felt like there was a hole inside me, and I was trying desperately to fill it – with money, women, alcohol, anything and everything. I wasn't happy in my own skin. I hated being alone; I couldn't just sit there, feeling at ease. And so whenever I was alone, I drank.' He developed physical problems too – his doctor told him that his liver, kidneys and pancreas were so badly damaged by alcohol that he might only have two years left to live.

Around this time he was going to Arizona to do a job remodelling houses, and an old girlfriend asked if she could travel with him. On the way, they stopped off in San Antonio, Texas to pick up her kids, who had been staying with their grandmother. Unfortunately his old girlfriend hadn't told him that she had given one of the kids up for adoption a few years before. Shortly after arriving in Arizona, they were both arrested on kidnapping charges. Bob was in jail for six weeks; it was the first time he'd ever stopped drinking, and he was forced to dry out in his cell. He went through delirium tremens, shaking so badly he had to sit on his hands and couldn't hold a coffee cup. He couldn't control his thoughts and was hallucinating, seeing spiders crawling over his body and wolves climbing through the bars of his cell.

But once the withdrawal from alcohol started to ease, he found he could think clearly for the first time in years, and realized that he wanted to stop drinking. He didn't want to die, didn't want to hate himself any more, and didn't want to keep ruining his businesses and his relationships. A couple of days later, the charges against him were dropped and he was released. He tried drinking one more time but nothing happened; he couldn't seem to get drunk. He started going to AA meetings every day and evening, and followed the 12-step programme as closely as he could. Nevertheless, it was a struggle. The craving for alcohol kept returning whenever his mind wasn't occupied or he had too much time on his hands. But finally, a year into his abstinence, he had a profound spiritual awakening which cured him of his craving. After an AA meeting, he was listening to a woman reading a passage from Og Mandino's *The Greatest Miracle in the World*. In Bob's own words:

The book was talking about God's love, about the blessings that he gives us, and right at that moment something inside me just opened up. I let go and God came into me. The woman told me later that I was literally glowing, like those old paintings where people have haloes around them. God just enveloped me in love. All this information started flowing into my brain, showing me that life was completely different to how I'd seen it before. I saw that God was an all-pervading force in everything. That consciousness was everywhere at all times. I felt this love in everything. I was in tune with the oneness of things; I felt at peace, in harmony. I was aware of the whole universe infinitely and of other dimensions of existence. All the highs I'd got from drugs or drinking – they were nothing compared to this.

The experience lasted a few days, but the craving lifted from me and has never come back. I've never had the desire to drink again. And since then I've been a different person. I feel comfortable in my own skin; I love being on my own. I have a sense of well-being all the time. Sometimes it makes other people angry. For example, last week after an AA meeting, a man said to me, 'It's easy for you - you're just sitting there so content and so relaxed!'

My relationships are so much better. I can see people as they really are; I recognize the God within them. I used to be so self-centred and selfish, but now I feel compassion and empathy. I want to help – that's why I'm alive. And it's when I'm helping people that the feeling of oneness and love comes back most strongly. It's always there, and I keep touching into it.

I see life as a journey now, not as a burden. I know there is God, but not the one taught by religions. The God of my understanding is the oneness of all, pure spirit consciousness, which is everywhere at all times.

In recent years, Bob's life hasn't been easy. After years of her own sobriety, his wife started drinking again, which led to their divorce. He has been laid off from work due to the recession, and has had to sell his house. But in his words, 'When bad things happen, I don't cling to them and let them upset me. I just let them go, and accept them as they are. I still want to get up each day. I'm still grateful to be alive, and to be sober, and to experience the world around me. I'm still happy.'

6

SPIRITUAL
TEACHERS

In view of the transformational power of suffering, it's not surprising that many well-known spiritual teachers went through periods of intense psychological turmoil before becoming teachers. Or to put it another way, it's not surprising that some of the people who undergo spiritual awakening after intense psychological turmoil go on to become spiritual teachers.

KRISHNAMURTI

This is true of one of the most famous spiritual teachers of the twentieth century, Jiddu Krishnamurti. His spiritual awakening seems to have been triggered by bereavement. He suffered a massive loss at the age of 10, with the death of his mother, whom he adored. Possibly because his parents were second cousins, their children were plagued by ill health, and 5 of Krishnamurti's 11 siblings died. (Krishnamurti suffered from ill health throughout his life too, although he lived to the age of 90.)

Krishnamurti had spiritual experiences as a child, characterized by what he called – speaking of himself in the third person – 'a strange lack of distance between himself and the trees, rivers and mountains'. At the age of 14, his 'spiritual potential' was recognized by members of the Theosophical Society, who took him under their wing, grooming him as the future 'world teacher'.

However, it wasn't until he was 27 years old that he underwent a permanent spiritual awakening. While visiting California, he started to experience terrible pain and discomfort, which lasted for two days. He became delirious, lost his appetite and finally seemed to become unconscious. But when he came to consciousness again, on the third day, the pain was gone and he realized that he was a different person. 'You don't know how I have changed,' he wrote to a friend at the time. 'My whole inner nature is alive with energy and thought.' He felt a new sense of mission, a desire to 'help the whole world to climb a few feet higher'.[1] He was filled with a profound sense of well-being, too, and no longer felt any separation. He was one with the whole cosmos:

Love in all its glory has intoxicated my heart; my heart can never be closed. I have drunk at the fountain of Joy and eternal Beauty. I am God-intoxicated...[2]

There was a man mending the road; that man was myself; the pickaxe he held was myself; the very stone which he was breaking up was part of me; the tender blade of grass was my very being, and the tree beside the man was myself... The birds, the dust, and the very noise were a part of me. Just then there was a car passing by at some distance; I was the driver, the

engine and the tyres... I was in everything, or rather
everything was in me, inanimate and animate, the
mountain, the worm and all breathing things.[3]

This transformation became firmly fixed three years later, when Krishnamurti's younger brother Nitya died of tuberculosis. The two of them were so close they were like twins. They were constant companions and Krishnamurti had spent much of the previous two years nursing his brother. At first he was devastated by the loss; a friend recalled how 'at night he would sob and moan and cry out for Nitya... Day after day we watched him, heartbroken, disillusioned.'[4] But at the same time as mourning his loss, Krishnamurti was, according to his friend, 'going through an inner revolution'.[5] His spiritual state intensified, and he felt a greater sense of compassion and a deeper inner strength:

An old dream is dead and a new one is being born, as
a flower that pushes through the solid earth. A new
vision is coming into being and a greater consciousness
is being unfolded. ... A new strength, born of suffering,
is pulsating in the veins and a new sympathy and
understanding is being born of past suffering – a
greater desire to see others suffer less, and, if they must
suffer, to see that they bear it nobly and come out of it
without too many scars. I have wept, but I do not want
others to weep; but if they do, I know what it means.[6]

With this new inner strength, Krishnamurti decided to break free of the Theosophical movement which had nurtured him since childhood. He renounced his role as the 'world teacher', declaring that 'truth is a pathless land' and that he didn't want to be part of any organization or accept any beliefs or dogma. For the rest of his life – another five and a half decades – he was an independent spiritual teacher, continually travelling, holding meetings and giving talks. His teachings are not easy to summarize – many people find them difficult even to understand – but his spiritual power was so great that millions of people gained a taste of enlightenment in his presence.

RUSSEL WILLIAMS

For the last 13 years, I have regularly visited a spiritual teacher called Russel Williams. He isn't widely known and has no desire to be. He has never published any writings or publicized himself. I recently suggested helping to put together a book of his teachings, together with stories from his life, but he was reluctant. 'I don't want a book published while I'm still alive,' he told me. However, he's happy for me to tell his story in short form here.

Russel was born in London in 1921. At the time of writing he is 89 years old, but looks and acts 25 years younger. He has an amazing amount of energy – he still walks and drives long distances, does all his own housework and spends long days gardening in the summer. Twice a week he drives 15 miles to the premises of the Buddhist Society of Manchester – which he has been the president of since 1978 – to hold talks. Even though I've been going to the meetings for 13 years, I still think of myself as a newcomer. Many people have been going there for 30 years or more. Even after all those years, Russel's teachings – and his presence – are still vibrant and powerful to them.

Even as a young child, Russel felt that he was 'aware of something powerful that I couldn't identify, but felt that I should know'. He recalls being aware that there was 'something more' at the age of nine, but his childhood and adolescence were so full of trauma and hardship that he didn't have the opportunity to investigate what it might be. His father was an invalid after being gassed during the First World War and his mother suffered from tuberculosis. His father died when he was 10, followed by his mother a year later. At that point his older brother, who was 12, joined the navy boys' service and his younger sister was taken in by an aunt. Russel's grandfather tried to get him into a Barnardo's children's home, but was told that he was too old. Left completely alone, Russel had no option but to leave school and start working, at the age of 11 and a half. His first job was on the shop floor of an engineering firm, then he went to Hull to work on trawlers and finally had a job at a tailor's shop back in London.

The loss of his family – his brother and sister as well as his parents – and the pressure of having to fend for himself at such a young age had left Russel in a desperate state. As with Krishnamurti, the spiritual awakening that came years later was probably partly the result of these bereavements. But for now, he reacted to them by becoming 'full of anger, with a hair-trigger temper. I felt a hatred towards myself, because of my ignorance, and it came out as aggression to others. I had a lot of fights and it's a wonder I didn't kill someone.'

The Second War World broke out when Russel was 18 and came at exactly the right time: 'Becoming a soldier saved me from a bad end, took me out of trouble. It taught me self-discipline and I learned how to control my emotions. It also took away the worry of keeping myself alive. It gave me regular food and shelter for the first time since my parents had died.'

Towards the end of May 1940, he had his first 48-hour leave pass and decided to go to London to see one of his aunts. As he was walking over Westminster Bridge, he saw a long trail of boats heading down the river Thames, and asked a man on a boat at the jetty what was happening. There was an emergency, he was told, and anyone who owned a boat had been ordered to sail it down to Chatham in Kent. Russel decided to go with the man on his boat. They crossed over the English Channel towards Dunkirk and took part in one of the most heroic and at the same time horrific events of the war: the evacuation of over a third of a million British and Allied soldiers from the French coast in the face of a barrage of bombings by the German Luftwaffe. Russel spent three days and nights ferrying soldiers from the beaches to larger destroyer ships, but has never talked in detail about what he saw there. 'I don't mind talking about anything else, but I can't talk about that,' he told me, his eyes welling up. 'The pain and suffering are impossible to describe. It showed the very worst and the very best in human nature.'

Just three months later, at the beginning of September 1940, Russel was stationed in London during the Blitz, when the Luftwaffe pulverized the city for 57 consecutive nights. It was his job to guard vulnerable points in the city, such as bridges and docks, and he hardly slept the whole time. 'It was incredibly stressful,' he says. 'By the end I felt as though I was having a nervous breakdown.'

In September 1942, Russel was wounded and decommissioned as a soldier. He became an electrician, working for the Air Ministry at an advanced airfield. It was during this time that he had a near-death experience when he was electrocuted:

I had to check the mains supply, but the insulation had broken down on the wire. I brushed against it and suddenly I was out of my body, miles up in space. I saw myself as a being of pure light. I knew I had two options, either to be reborn or to go back and get my body going

*again. Without any words being spoken, it was known
that there was work to be done, that I had to return. And
fortunately there was no permanent damage.*

At the time of D-Day, in June 1944, when Allied troops landed
in France, Russel had another very traumatic experience. He
was on his own at the airfield, acting as duty manager, and a
security clampdown meant that there was nobody to relieve
him as manager and that no food could get through to the
airfield. Russel was on his own for three days and nights,
working around the clock without food or sleep, until he
collapsed with exhaustion.

When the war ended a year later, Russel was, as he
describes it, 'an automaton, emotionally and physically a
washout'. Initially, he was going to start an electrical repair
business with a colleague, but found it impossible to settle
down. He became a tramp for several months, drifting from
town to town and job to job until he ended up working in a
travelling circus, looking after horses. He did this for three
and a half years and it became a kind of spiritual training
for him. He found that in order to understand the animals,
he just had to observe them, not think or form any opinions
about them. He noticed how they responded to subtle
changes in his mood and behaviour, and found that they
responded best when he was wholly present. If his mind was
on other things and he didn't give them his full attention,
they became agitated. But if he was fully *there*, calm and
alert, they became calm too. As a result, he cultivated a quiet
mind and learned to live wholly in the moment.

And one day when he was with a horse in the stables, he
had his first powerful spiritual awakening:

*I turned to look at the horse, which had steam coming
out of its nose. And all of a sudden I became it. I was
inside it. I could look through its eyes and mind. I was*

aware of its true nature. I was aware that all things were one. I also realized that I had profound peace within me.

I went to the hangar, where the lion was, and I was one with him too. Then one of the dogs. Then I was all of them and they were all one. They were only separate in terms of form and structure. It was the same essence, the same emptiness, in all of them.

As with so many of the experiences we've heard, this spiritual experience was the onset of a permanent change of being, a psychological transformation. Afterwards Russel was a different person. The anger that had been simmering inside him since he was a child faded away and never returned. The chattering of his ego halted, so that his mind was always clear and empty. He lost the sense of separation from others and the world around him. As he put it, 'I no longer experienced desire or aversion. I was at peace with myself.'

After this, Russel felt a constant rapport with the animals he worked with, and with other human beings. Animals that were agitated and aggressive with others became calm and cooperative with him. For example, once a horse stepped on broken glass; the glass was embedded in its hoof and it was screaming in pain. It wouldn't stand still for long enough for anyone to help it until Russel arrived. In his presence it calmed down and became so still that he was able to lift up its hoof, find the broken glass underneath all the blood and take out the pieces.

People started to come to him with their problems too, as if they knew they could tell them to him without being judged. He sometimes didn't even need to speak – somehow they benefited from the calmness of his presence and the full attention he gave them.

However, this wasn't the end of Russel's struggles. Like Janice, who had a similar experience of oneness with a seabird and a horse, he didn't have a framework to help him understand his transformation. This was the early 1950s, when there was little knowledge of spiritual traditions or practices in the West. Russel tried to talk to people about what had happened to him, to describe how his vision of the world had changed, but met with complete incomprehension. People thought he was mad, and he started to believe them. He started to doubt himself, to question the value of the insights he'd been given, and began to feel frustrated again. However, this led to another powerful spiritual experience which dissolved his doubts and firmly established his new spiritual state:

> There was something inside me that had to come out but wouldn't. I was pushing it further and further away. Eventually I shouted out, 'Somebody help me!' It was if somebody dropped a blanket over me. I've never known such peace in all my life. It lasted three days... There was a sense of freedom. And that freedom and peace have remained inside me right until now.

By this time, in 1957, Russel was working as an attendant at a swimming baths in Islington, back in London (the circus had gone to Ireland and he'd decided not to go with it). One night, on his way back to his flat, he bought a newspaper and opened it at a tiny advert for a talk about spiritual healing. He felt strangely compelled to go, but the meeting was disappointing – the 'healer' was obviously a charlatan. At the end, a man two rows in front of him stood up and gave the healer a dressing-down, saying, 'If you think this is spiritual healing, you must be out of your mind.' Then he turned round to Russel and said, 'I didn't come for that, so you must be the reason I'm here.'

The man was called John Garrie, one of the founders of the Buddhist Society of Great Britain. That evening Russel described his realization experience and the vision of the world it had given him, and Garrie exclaimed, 'That's pure Buddhism!' Russel had barely heard of Buddhism and certainly knew nothing about it, and Garrie was astounded to find that someone so untutored had attained realization purely through his own efforts. He introduced Russel to the other members of the society and Russel started to give talks there. They adopted him as their teacher – and so began his long life as a spiritual teacher. On New Year's Eve 1957, he travelled up to Manchester to meet the members of the Buddhist Society of Manchester (also founded by John Garrie, in 1951), and has been there ever since.

Russel teaches a form of *advaita*, or non-duality. He tells us that consciousness is the fundamental reality of the universe, the 'unmanifest' which gives rise to the whole visible material world. That consciousness also expresses itself as the individual consciousness of human beings. At the essence of our beings, we are one with the universe – and with all other beings and all other forms – because we consist of the same essence. Russel teaches that the nature of consciousness is bliss and oneness, and that it's only the activity of the ego – its constant chattering and its desires – that stops us experiencing those qualities. In order to help recover our true nature, he recommends self-observation and mindfulness practices.

However, as anyone who attends his meetings will tell you, it isn't just Russel's teachings which are so striking and powerful, but also his *presence*. As I describe in *Waking from Sleep*, a powerful spiritual radiance emanates from him, which can induce spiritual experiences in anyone who is receptive.

ECKHART TOLLE

Russel's experience is strikingly similar to Eckhart Tolle's. Eckhart's spiritual awakening even occurred at exactly the same age as Russel's, 29.

Until that time Eckhart had lived in an almost continual state of depression and anxiety. Interviewed for this book, he described it to me as follows:

> *A high state of anxiety, a state of depression, existential despair and anguish. There was a sense of great fear of life: fear of the future, fear of the meaninglessness underneath it all, but not wanting to fully face that meaninglessness and find out what underlay it. I remember reading* Nausea *by Jean-Paul Sartre. There were some things there that I recognized: the feeling that the world was alien, almost hostile. Even inanimate objects felt hostile. The feeling was especially severe at night – waking up and feeling the alien nature of the walls surrounding you, even the furniture, a sense of complete separateness from one's surroundings, of great aloneness. Not solitude, which is something positive, but aloneness, the feeling of being cut off. You're floating around on the shore of reality as a meaningless fragment that's been torn out of some larger whole which once made sense.*

Although Eckhart's depression was mainly caused by internal psychological factors, there were some external factors too. One was his parents' unhappy marriage and the continual conflict between them. He had also been unhappy at school, where he had felt like an outsider:

> *I didn't fit in. I remember my closest friend at school had a severe physical handicap. Most people didn't want to have anything to do with him. I was an outsider for inner reasons and he was an outsider for physical reasons. The sense of not fitting in was always there. There was something within me that prevented me from being a part of the normal world. For a while I seemed to fit in at university, but later on, when I did graduate work, I realized that I didn't belong there either.*

> *Later I considered suicide as an escape several times, but those thoughts were there even when I was a child. I remember when I was 10 we lived in a house with scaffolding, because the façade was being painted. The scaffolding was up for a few weeks and I remember thinking 'That's good. If ever I need to jump down it will be easy – I can just climb up the scaffolding.'*

Another external factor was Eckhart's lack of social roots. After his parents separated when he was 13, he moved countries twice, first to Spain and then to England. At first moving to England was a positive step; his father had married again and 'It was quite a relief to no longer be a part of my father's unhappy marriage.' But although Eckhart worked – as a language teacher – for his first three years in England, he felt very lonely:

> *I didn't have family here and didn't know anybody. I loved England; I felt closer to England than I did to any other country. Nevertheless, I felt a sense of isolation,*

especially in London. I lived in bedsits for the first few years; I enjoyed walking the streets but I always had to come back to my bedsit at night.

Along with the anguish and isolation, there was a feeling of inadequacy, of wanting to be somebody and to show the world that I was someone. It was unconscious. When people need to boost their sense of self they usually look to the most obvious thing, the thing they can identify with most strongly. Some people might have good looks, physical strength, a good body, family background, possessions, but I didn't have any of those things. There wasn't much I could identify with. What was left for me was intelligence. I became interested in intellectual things – it was partly a search for an answer in the intellectual realm and partly an attempt to strengthen my sense of identity as someone who was quite knowledgeable. There was an ego aspect which took the form of reading psychology and philosophy in my early and mid-twenties. At that time I thought the human mind had the answer and that I could find it by studying philosophy.

I got into university quite late and had an exaggerated view of what university was like. I thought the professors had the answer – but I began to realize that they were just as unhappy as anybody else. As I describe in A New Earth, *one professor I really admired committed suicide. The professors were just as unhappy as I was. The intellectual realm didn't supply any true answers, just more questions.*

The more I pursued my intellectual search, the stronger the sense of despair became. On the other hand, I continued with it because it gave me an illusory sense of identity. In my own eyes and in the eyes of the world I became a kind of intellectual and there was an ego satisfaction in that. But in every ego satisfaction there is always the fear that it's not enough. The more you strengthen your ego, the more the sense of fear grows, the fear of not being good enough. The more you present a façade of confidence to the outside world, the greater the unconscious fear grows. That's why people need to play roles. They don't realize that they are already enough.

The ego grew and the despair grew during my twenties. I was extremely anxious to do well at university, and although I was depressed at the time, I was working very hard. A few years ago I met a friend I was at university with and he said, 'You were always working. You always stayed up late studying.' But my motivation wasn't a joyful thing – it was the fear of not being good enough, the fear of needing to prove that I could be better than others. My motivation was anxiety.

In the finals I got a first-class degree and for a few weeks I felt very happy. But then the anxiety came back – what do I do now? There was the beginning of the realization that my anxiety wasn't caused by external things and would carry on no matter what I achieved.

In retrospect, the unhappiness arose from an inner state of disconnectedness. When everything breaks down around you, it brings out this latent sense of disconnectedness that is already there, in everybody, the sense of not being rooted in yourself, of being out of contact with the source of life. As long as things are going well around you, without any major breakdown, there's a slight sense of fear, of anxiety, which people cover up. But when things start breaking down, the cover-up no longer works.

This can happen with people who seem to have everything. They have fame, money and can go anywhere and do anything, but it's no longer fulfilling; they can't cover up their inner sense of disconnectedness and separation. When external events become negative, you feel the emptiness within more strongly.

For Eckhart himself, the emptiness within – and his general sense of anxiety and despair – became so strong that one night when he was 29, he woke up with the overpowering desire to kill himself. The thought 'I cannot live with myself any longer' kept running through his mind, until he suddenly realized that this statement meant there were *two* of him, a self that was suffering and a self that was standing back and observing the suffering self. And right at that moment a dis-identification occurred. His identity withdrew from his fictitious ego self and its story, and that self immediately dissolved away, leaving a sense of pure being and pure peace.

Initially he was afraid, but he obeyed an inner voice which told him to 'resist nothing'. He felt that there was a kind of black hole inside him, a vortex of energy drawing him down – and then his fear melted away and the next thing he knew it was morning.

On waking, he felt he was a new person, living in a new world. He was in a state of wonder and bliss. As he describes it in *The Power of Now*, 'I walked around the city in utter amazement at the miracles of life on earth, as if I had just been born into this world.'[7]

He didn't know what had happened to him, just that he felt an amazing sense of peace. At first he thought it might just be a temporary experience, but as the days and weeks went by without it fading away, he began to realize that it was permanent.

Although he wasn't completely aware of it at the time, one of the major psychological changes Eckhart had undergone was that his mind had become quiet; the ego's incessant 'thought-chatter' had stopped. As he told me:

When the transformation first happened, all I knew was that I was peaceful. I didn't know why. But my mind had slowed down. It was far less active. There were long periods in my daily life where there was no thinking or very little thinking or only important thinking. I was no longer identified with thought processes. Those compulsive automatic processes had subsided – the noisy mind which I had identified with, which had covered up the deeper dimension within me. But at the time, I didn't know that directly, only through the peace that I felt.

I was also much more aware of beauty. The world around me was no longer perceived as threatening, it was perceived as being alive. There was a great sense of appreciation of the little things – not just the spectacular beauty of a flowering tree, but the beauty of even the most insignificant objects, even inanimate objects. But I felt the beauty of natural phenomena very strongly, and appreciated their beingness, and their presence.

I no longer felt separateness between myself and the world around me. I felt a oneness with my surroundings, inanimate and animate. That also meant that people were no longer perceived as threatening. Before that shift I felt that when I met people, there was some kind of fear in the background. When I walked into a room I felt uneasy. But now I could relate to human beings with a sense of ease. I no longer had to prove anything.

The important part of that is not needing to continually label one's perceptions. I was able to look at things without attaching labels to them, calling them something. I didn't interpret human beings, just let them be as they were. The mental compulsion is to immediately define and interpret everything you perceive. Stopping that brings about a great sense of ease and oneness – the compulsion to label everything makes reality something abstract and mental. When everything is immediately labelled and interpreted, you live in a reality which is conceptualized. You are full of viewpoints and opinions, and whatever you perceive is immediately filtered through viewpoints and opinions and you completely identify with them. Without the compulsion to interpret things, there is a freedom of perception – that's why it's called liberation. The world comes to life suddenly.

Although he was very well read, Eckhart had little knowledge of spiritual states or traditions and so didn't understand what had happened to him:

Being able to talk about it to others, to explain it to others, let alone help them – that came years later. A sudden awakening doesn't mean a sudden understanding. I only knew I was at peace and I didn't know why. But because I felt at peace, I felt very drawn to investigating spiritual teachings and schools and religions. I felt an affinity with them. When I listened to a true spiritual teacher or read some true spiritual teachings, I felt an elation inside, a recognition. There was inner knowing that told me, 'There's truth.' I recognized it when it came from a true source, not a second-hand one.

So I read the Bhagavad-Gita, *the* Tao Te Ching *and the Gospels, and I recognized a core of truth that I hadn't seen before. I visited Buddhist monasteries in England. I listened to Buddhist monks, especially one or two who were in touch with the source. They explained to me the essential teachings of Buddhism and told me about the illusion of self,* anatta. *A monk said to me, 'Zen is all about stopping thinking.' This was already three or four years after my transformation and I realized that that was what had happened to me. In the New Testament it says, 'Deny thyself.' That must imply that the self is unreal, because if the self were real it would be absurd to deny it. It ultimately means recognizing the unreality of the sense of self.*

Eckhart became a spiritual teacher almost by accident, simply because people were drawn to his peaceful presence. They began to come to him with their questions and problems and he found that the answers seemed to arise naturally within him:

I noticed a great intensification of presence in those situations, in teaching situations. People who came to me with questions could feel that too and they sometimes asked, 'What's happening? I can feel this energy, this peace.' That's part of the energy which comes with spiritual teaching. The words can be important, but may be only secondary. The energy field is more important than the words. It gradually came to me that people felt drawn towards that.

Occasionally it happens that people perceive you as something special. They want to make you into something special. This is a pitfall for anyone who becomes a spiritual teacher. It's in them, but they think it's coming from you. It's actually something that arises between you and them. I always need to point out that it doesn't come from me, this increase in presence.

It has now been more than 30 years since Eckhart's transformation, and his shift in identity has been permanent. His awakened state has never faded, although there are sometimes fluctuations in its intensity:

Sometimes the underlying peace is just in the background; at other times it becomes so all-encompassing that it almost obliterates sensory perceptions and thoughts and what one would usually consider one's life. Even when things in the foreground might seem turbulent, in the background there is some sense of stillness and peace.

It's the opposite to what you might expect. When there is a critical situation, the peace suddenly becomes intensified. When everything is going well, it can recede into the background. The dimmer switch can be at different settings, but the light is always on!

As a result of his own experiences, Eckhart is fully aware of the spiritual potential of trauma and turmoil and the radical transformation they can bring:

Most people need the unreality of the sense of self. It's so strongly established that they need to be hit by suffering for it to be broken. Sometimes even that is not enough. But even if the suffering just causes a crack in the rigid shell of the self, then suddenly you become open to spiritual teachings. It may not bring about a complete awakening, but it accelerates the inner transformation.

When things break down, one's artificial sense of self breaks down too. One had identified with something outside, whether a possession, a close relationship or your body. The forms eventually collapse and when they do, identification with form is shaken. That is suffering. One's sense of self is no longer solid and dissolves. The positive aspect of that is that there's something more real in its place.

Suffering is not always a guarantee of inner transformation. Often it is resisted so fiercely that the ego actually grows, and people become embittered and angry with themselves or with the world. The ego becomes very rigid and you become full of resentment. The transformation may not happen until your deathbed, and even then you could still be angry, so suffering is always an opportunity, but often it's not taken.

BYRON KATIE

Another modern spiritual teacher, Byron Katie, had a very similar experience. She experienced intense psychological turmoil for almost a decade, hating herself so much – and so convinced that everyone else hated her too – that she continually thought about committing suicide. She self-medicated with codeine and alcohol to try to escape her self-loathing, and developed an eating disorder too. During the last two years of her depression she was also agoraphobic and rarely left her bedroom.

Eventually Katie was admitted into a residential treatment centre for women with eating disorders. At first she was angry and upset, and resisted the idea of treatment. But after two weeks, she experienced a sudden psychological shift. One morning she woke up to the sensation of a cockroach crawling across her foot. And as she opened her eyes, it was as if a new self had woken up with her. She felt that she was suddenly looking at the world through new eyes. This new self was so distinct from her old that she had no memory of her previous life. She didn't even recognize her husband or children and had to relearn social conventions.

This new self existed in a state of intense well-being and fullness, with a heightened intensity of perception, a freedom from anxiety, an acceptance of reality and a constant sense of appreciation and well-being. And it has never faded. Ever since that time – 15 years ago at the time of writing – this self has been permanent and constant:

> *Just to see my hand in front of my face, or my foot, or the table, or anything, it's to see it for the first time. Here are the words that I would use: 'It's a privilege beyond what can be told.' It's self experiencing the mirror image of itself...*

I only know that I have not seen a problem in 13 years [at the time of writing] that is real. And I have not met anyone or anything that I would change. Everything brings me such joy. I am everything. If that's what a sustained transcendent experience is, no wonder people seek it; even though it is always, always apparent.[8]

Katie no longer has a sense of ego-separateness. The boundaries of her ego have disappeared, so that she experiences a constant sense of oneness with the world. Her sense of identity spreads beyond her own body and mind, to include her surroundings: 'When I'm driving in a car, everything's coming into me. It ends there. I am the beginning and the end of all of it.' Rather than being 'physically grounded in my body', she is 'Everywhere. Everywhere your eyes see.'[9]

After Katie's transformation, people started to be attracted to her, as they were to Russel and Eckhart. They wanted to be in her presence, to tell her their problems, and slowly she became a spiritual teacher too. She now devotes her life to travelling the world giving demonstrations of what she calls 'The Work', a system by which people can observe and analyse their own thinking and become free of negative and self-limiting thoughts.

CATHERINE INGRAM

Catherine Ingram, author of *Passionate Presence*, also became a spiritual teacher after a long period of turmoil. Like Russel Williams, her early life was filled with suffering. Her childhood was so unhappy that by the age of four she had a stress-induced stomach ulcer. She became a seeker at the age of 12, in an attempt to make sense of the world, to understand why it could be so unjust. She studied the texts of Eastern philosophy and practised Buddhist meditation for many years, at the same time as travelling the world in search of intense experience and wisdom. As a journalist for spiritual and mind, body, spirit magazines, she interviewed many famous spiritual teachers and social activists, including the Dalai Lama and Krishnamurti, in the hope of absorbing some of their serenity and wisdom.

Catherine had many profound and powerful experiences, but there was still something missing. There was always a gnawing hunger inside which impelled her to keep searching, but which was never satisfied. As she describes it, 'The problem was that no matter how satisfied and alive I felt in moments of profound experience, it didn't last. Like the hunger that returns only hours after the gourmet meal ... the experience of fulfilment was limited by time.'[10]

Another problem, she realized later, was that ultimately her desire for fulfilment was ego-driven. She was striving to add something to herself, to become someone better or higher. This also meant that she was living for the future rather than in the present. Even when she did feel intensely alive, she wasn't experiencing the state fully – half her mind was already in the future, aware that the state was going to end at some point soon and thinking about how she would savour it later.

After years of this striving, Catherine fell deeply in love. She was engaged to be married and felt she had finally found fulfilment in the relationship. But her hopes ended in despair when her fiancé left her for another woman. It was a devastating blow, a combination of loss and betrayal, and led to further losses. Because the man had been very rich, she had let go of her work and lost contact with the magazines and newspaper she had worked for earlier. Since she had lived with the man, she had no home of her own and had to stay with friends. As she told me, 'I found myself quite destitute, with no money, nowhere to live, no car, no prospects and no work or income. And in the future it looked like I was going to be truly homeless.'

But, as was the case with Kevin, being stripped of everything in this way led to spiritual rebirth. The destruction of her identity allowed a new self to be born. Or as she describes it, the suffering was 'like the burning-up of thick veils which had been obscuring true seeing, for a long time'.[11]

However, unlike the other transformations we've looked at in this chapter, Catherine's was gradual and is still ongoing. It was particularly strong during the few months when she was still traumatized by the break-up. Because her future was so full of fear and her past so full of loss, she was forced to focus wholly on the present as a way of escaping the pain. And through this – just as Russel learned to be present-centred through working with animals – she learned the habit of being wholly attentive to her present experience. As she told me:

There comes a point where there are only two options left – you either go insane or you become clear. I had enough support to manage the intensity of the feelings and keep directing my attention to the present. Any step into the past led me into feelings of regret, so I was forced just to be here and now. There was no place I could be in peace except in present awareness, clear of all thinking and ruminating.

I had a sense of just allowing things to arise while sitting in a big space, allowing anything to come and go, with no resistance. It was like sitting with an old close friend. I found that reality was perfectly fine.

As with Russel, this habit became more established over time. She describes this as 'not fighting with reality. When emotions arise or events occur, you just let them be and sense the space around them. There's an acceptance of every moment, a continual merging with reality, with *just this*.'

Shortly after this, in 1992, at the invitation of Ram Dass, Catherine became a spiritual teacher, holding 'Dharma Dialogues' throughout the United States, Europe and Australia and leading silent retreats several times a year.

Several years ago, she experienced another highly traumatic event that deepened this state of presence. Soon after her book *Passionate Presence* was completed, her younger brother died. This was a much bigger loss than the end of her relationship, as he was like a son as well as a brother to her. He was 12 years younger and she had raised him. As she describes it:

The grief was huge; the only thing to do was to feel the space around it, to feel the loss and deeply surrender to the very fact of it. Rather than telling a story about how it should not have happened, how he was too young to die, you find yourself in a kind of quiet acceptance, even though the pain is intense. You have to let it be. It's like a thunderstorm in an open sky: no matter how big it becomes, it's still happening in that space.

When my brother died, I could feel the enormous context in which life and death happen, the universality of loss and of death itself. It created a clarity in my awareness that had not been there before.

There's really little difference between these teachers' transformational experiences and the others we've read about. Perhaps the only real difference is one of degree. I've already suggested that there are different degrees of spiritual awakening, and perhaps – as a general rule – it's the individuals who experience higher degrees of awakening who go on to become spiritual teachers.

This is certainly not always the case, though. In a sense, any of the awakened individuals we've heard from could become spiritual teachers, and it's true that some of them – like Jamie, or Stephanie and Glyn, or Michael – have become awakened to quite an intense degree. So perhaps it's a question of inclination too. Or it may simply be that these spiritual teachers managed to understand and integrate their spiritual transformation to a high degree, whereas others, like Jamie or Stephanie, may still be in the process of adapting to their new identity and other people's responses to them. In fact, Glyn told me that now she's almost ready to tell other people about her transformation and to try to help them in their own spiritual development.

It's also important to point out that in most cases – certainly in Eckhart's, Russel's and Byron Katie's – there isn't a conscious decision to become a spiritual teacher. Eckhart and Russel became spiritual teachers because other people recognized their enlightened state and were drawn to them. And this raises the question of how you define the term 'spiritual teacher'. In a sense, everyone who becomes awakened is a teacher in that everyone around them benefits from their serenity and wisdom.

PART II

DEATH: THE GREAT **AWAKENER**

7

THE PARADOX
OF DEATH

Imagine that there was one experience that was guaranteed to permanently wake people up, or at least that had a good chance of doing so. Imagine that, after this experience, people would have a permanent sense of wonder and appreciation, a sense of the harmony and meaning of the universe, and a strong sense of connection to it.

Believe it or not, this experience already exists, although only a small number of people have been privileged to have it so far: a journey to the moon, or into space. A large proportion of the 24 American astronauts who travelled to the moon in the late 1960s and early '70s had powerful spiritual experiences during their trip and were permanently transformed as a result. A term has even been invented for the phenomenon: 'lunar consciousness'.

Jim Irvin was a member of the first extended scientific expedition to the moon in August 1971. When he returned to Earth after his two weeks in space he found that he could appreciate everything – all the mundane and ordinary activities of life he had completely taken for granted before. He found that just to sit in a chair or to eat food in the normal way was a source of joy. He felt that he had found the perfect cure for anybody who was prone to depression and boredom: just shut them in a box and deprive them of all ordinary experience for two weeks then let them out again.

But that wasn't the most the most important part of his experience. Before his trip, Irvin had been a conventional church-going Christian. He'd thought of God as a personal being who existed apart from the world and controlled it from somewhere else in the universe. But while he was on the moon he felt that God was there with him. He experienced God as a living presence which pervaded the whole of the universe and everything in it. The experience affected him so profoundly that just a few months after his return to Earth, he left NASA and spent the rest of his life as a evangelist.

Charlie Duke, a member of the *Apollo 16* mission in April 1972, had a similar experience. While looking out from the hatch of the spaceship onto the lunar landscape, he had a mystical vision of the presence of the divine. As he describes it, 'I was overwhelmed by the certainty that what I was witnessing was part of the universality of God.' While walking on the moon and looking down at his fresh footprints in the lunar dust, he 'just choked up. Tears came. It was the most deeply moving experience of my life.'[1] He'd never been particularly interested in religion or spirituality before, but shortly after his return to Earth he also became a born again Christian. As he puts it, his three days' walk on the moon led to a walk with Jesus for eternity.

Edgar Mitchell also had a mystical experience, but didn't interpret it in conventional religious terms. He was a member of the third successful mission to the moon in January 1971 and holds the joint record for the longest moonwalk (9 hours and 17 minutes). While looking out at the Earth from his spaceship, he felt an overpowering sense of euphoria and tranquillity and shifted into a different state of consciousness in which he perceived the meaning of the universe. There was nothing accidental; the universe was filled with order and harmony. And there was no separateness. All planets and stars and all human beings were a part of the same whole, part of a spiritual force which pervaded the whole universe. He was a part of this unity too. He wasn't a detached observer looking at it from the outside, he was inside it; in fact he *was* it.

This feeling returned to Mitchell several times during the journey home, in fact every time he looked at the Earth. He felt that he'd become enlightened in some way, although he didn't fully understand what had happened. He described it later as 'the overview effect' and summarized the experience as 'interconnected euphoria' and 'instant global consciousness'.[2]

The experience changed the course of Mitchell's life. He turned his attention from outer to *inner* space. He began to read books on spirituality and consciousness and to do research on altered states of consciousness and psychic phenomena. Within two years of his trip to the moon, he had left NASA and set up his own research institute, the Institute of Noetic Sciences, which is still flourishing today.

Gene Cerman, who took part in two lunar missions – *Apollo 10* and *16* – had a similar vision of meaning and purpose. As he describes it in the film *In the Shadow of the Moon*:

> I was standing on a plateau somewhere out there in
> space that science and technology had allowed me
> to get to. But now what I was seeing, and even more
> importantly what I was feeling at that moment in

time, science and technology had no answers for...
Because there I was and there you are, the Earth –
dynamic, overwhelming – and I felt the world was just
... there was too much purpose, too much logic. It was
too beautiful to happen by accident. There has to be
somebody bigger than you, and bigger than me, and
I mean this in a spiritual sense, not a religious sense.
There has to be a creator of the universe who stands
above the religions that we ourselves create to go on in
our lives.[3]

Another astronaut who experienced personal transformation was Al Worden, a member of *Apollo 15* in July 1971. He had always thought of himself as a fairly normal man, rational and extraverted. He'd never been particularly sensitive or emotional, and had certainly never written – or even read – any poetry. But as he was orbiting the moon, something shifted inside him. On his return to Earth he started to write soul-searching poetry to express his feelings about the miracle of his journey into space. Reflecting on his journey to the moon, he wrote,

> *In love with myself and with my work*
> *Unheeding the many dangers that lurk*
> *In outer space or here on earth*
> *I accept all as due my birth.*[4]

Rusty Schweikhart didn't actually travel to the moon – he was a member of the *Apollo 9* mission, in March 1969, which carried out tests to prepare for the moon landings later that year. But his vision of the Earth from space also transformed him.

One of the tests was a spacewalk around his lunar module, where he floated 160 miles above the Earth and just a few miles above the moon. As he gazed below, he felt as though he had lost his identity as an American astronaut and was 'part of everyone and everything sweeping past me below'. And he felt a profound attachment to and appreciation for the planet Earth:

> *You realize that on that small spot, that little blue and*
> *white planet, is everything that means anything to you*
> *– all of the history and music and poetry and art and*
> *death and birth and love, tears, joys, games, all of it on*
> *that little spot out there... This tiny beautiful Earth –*
> *the planet that keeps us alive, that gives us everything*
> *we have, the food we eat, the water we drink, the air*
> *we breathe, the beauty of nature. And everything is so*
> *perfectly balanced and organized so that we can live.*
> *This beautiful tiny planet spinning through space.*[5]

This heightened state of awareness stayed with Rusty after his return to Earth and his life changed as a result. Whereas before he'd given little thought to anything beyond his career as an astronaut, his new sense of connection filled him with the need to help others. He started to do voluntary work at a clinic for drug addicts and as a telephone counsellor for troubled teenagers, and also to practise transcendental meditation.

Many astronauts felt this profound gratitude for the Earth and later became involved in environmental causes as a result. Alan Bean, the fourth man to walk on the moon, has found that his appreciation of the wonder of life on Earth has never faded in 40 years:

> *Since that time I have not complained about the*
> *weather a single time. I'm glad there is weather. I've*
> *not complained about traffic – I'm glad there are*

*people around. ...When I got back home, I [would go]
down to shopping centres and I'd just go around there,
get an ice cream or something, and just watch the
people go by and think, 'Boy, we're lucky to be here.'
Why do people complain about the Earth? We are
living in the garden of Eden!*[6]

With the possible exception of Ed Mitchell, none of these astronauts had any interest in unusual states of consciousness beforehand. They were hard-headed scientists who even had a reputation for being emotionless automatons. It wasn't as though they went looking for these experiences either – every minute of their time in space was meticulously planned out, filled with tests and tasks, so they had little opportunity to relax and contemplate their situation. Nevertheless, space travel gave them what millions of monks and seekers have been searching for since time immemorial: a taste of enlightenment and a shift to a new state of being.

It's perhaps a shame, then, that space travel isn't yet available to members of the public. Seeing our planet from space would have a similar awakening and life-changing effect on all of us. Gazing at the oasis of the Earth with the whole universe still and silent around us, we'd be likely to see *Erahman* pervading the whole universe and experience our oneness with it.

This would be impossible, of course, but in a sense it's also unnecessary, because there is one experience we all have which can be, if approached in the right way, the equivalent of travelling to the moon: facing our own death.

It's sometimes said that human beings are the only animals who are aware of their own death, but is this really true?

Many of us live our life almost as if there's no such thing as death, putting things off and never taking any chances or feeling any urgency, as if we have an infinite amount of time on our hands. We damage and pollute our bodies as if we're indestructible and take life itself for granted just as we largely take our health, freedom and the people in our life for granted.

Part of the reason for this is that many of us don't *want* to think about death. We live in a death-denying culture; if sex was the great taboo of the twentieth century, then death is the great taboo of the late twentieth and early twenty-first. At earlier times, people made a conscious effort to remind themselves of their own mortality, through *memento mori* (literally, 'remember you must die'). In the sixteenth century, scholars used to keep skulls on their desks to remind them that they were always close to death, while in the Victorian era people wore lockets containing the hair of their deceased loved ones, and mourning veils. But, perhaps because of our materialistic, youth-worshipping culture, and because many of us don't believe in an afterlife, we try to repress our awareness of death.

But this is a great shame, because if confronted directly, becoming aware of our own mortality can be a liberating and awakening experience. We've already seen – for example with Glyn and Stephanie – that the death of people close to us can trigger transformational experiences (or SITEs, as I'll refer to them from now on, standing for 'suffering-induced transformational experiences'.) And when we face death *personally*, the effect is even more powerful.

Of course, some of the experiences we've looked at so far have featured personal encounters with death: for example, Cheryl, Carrie and Iris had to face the possibility that they were going to die of cancer, while Gill Hicks and Michael Hutchison both had near-death experiences. However, in this section of the book we're going to look at experiences where encountering death was the *main* factor, or even the only one. In this chapter, we're going to look at the cases of people who experienced awakening as they went through the process of dying. Then in the following two chapters, we're going to look at people who returned from both long-term and sudden encounters with death.

DENNIS POTTER

How do you think you'd feel if you had a fatal disease and only had a certain amount of time to live? You'd probably expect to be devastated and depressed, thinking about all the friends and relatives you were leaving behind, and all the things you planned to do with the rest of your life but wouldn't be able to do now. You might think about the things in your life that you'd worked so hard to build up but were now going to be taken away from you. It might seem monstrously unfair, having to die while everyone else was living on.

However, there's a chance that you might react in a much more positive way. There's even a chance that the process of dying would be a serene and even blissful experience.

The English playwright Dennis Potter, famous for television plays like *The Singing Detective*, was, by all accounts, not a particularly likeable person throughout most of his life. He was a short-tempered and bitter man who had at least as many enemies as friends. But during the final months of his life, after he'd learned that he was dying of prostate cancer, his character changed. He became serene and compassionate, and admitted that his coldness and aggression had really only been a mask he'd used to hide his natural timidity. During a TV interview he gave shortly before his death, he remarked that he didn't feel sad or sorry for himself, only for the close friends and family who were going to be losing somebody they loved. He said that he was, in fact, happier and more at peace with the world than he'd ever been before. The knowledge that he was going to die soon generated a state of inner well-being, together with a heightened awareness of his surroundings, an intense awareness of the 'nowness' of his experience and the beautiful 'is-ness' of the world. As he said during the interview:

> We forget that life can only be defined in the present tense. It is, is, is. And it is now only...

> That nowness becomes so vivid to me that in a perverse sort of way I'm serene. I can celebrate life... The nowness of everything is absolutely wonderful... The fact is that if you see, in the present tense – boy, can you see it; boy, can you celebrate it.[7]

Things he'd seen millions of times before now seemed amazingly beautiful and full of significance, as if it was the first time he'd really seen them. Looking through the window at apple blossom in his garden, it seemed to him 'the whitest, frothiest, blossomiest blossom that there ever could be'.[8]

In other words, Dennis Potter's imminent death brought about a psychological transformation, a shift to a higher state of consciousness. And this wasn't just a temporary experience, but a stable, continuous state which apparently lasted for weeks until his death.

PILGRIMS

In his recent book *Pilgrims*, a hospice nurse called Paul McDermott describes his relationship with a lady named Val, who was dying of cancer. When he first met her, she was 74 years old and had been given a month to live. She was an ordinary working-class woman who had barely had an education and hardly ever read books. She had spent most of her working life in a post office and been married to an army engineer, who had died four years before.

The charity Paul worked for offered support for people who wanted to die in their own homes and he drove out to see Val two or three times a week. At first, he found her difficult and hostile. Although she had agreed to the support, she seemed reluctant to cooperate, or even be civil to him. She seemed to enjoy embarrassing him, trying to make him feel uncomfortable by asking, 'So, do you think I'm dying?' Knowing that he'd come to the UK from New Zealand a few years earlier, she would complain about 'foreigners flooding into Britain'.

Paul began to realize that this wasn't just him, though – Val seemed to be difficult with everyone. She had fallen out with all her family, including her only child, and didn't seem able to keep any friends.

However, as Paul gained her trust, and as she began to accept her imminent death, her personality changed, like Dennis Potter's. She began to read poetry – a copy of the *Rubaiyat* of Omar Khayam, a present from her husband years before – and together, Paul and Val started to explore how she felt about dying. They discussed philosophical questions such as whether there was life after death and whether God existed. Then, one day while cooking, Val had a sudden mystical experience:

I was making a little roast: some potatoes and beans and a nice bit of chicken. And then suddenly I just stopped. The kitchen knife was in my hand in mid-air ... and I just stopped. I didn't move for I don't know how long. It might have been a minute, it might have been an hour, I don't know, but I knew time didn't matter... While I was standing there I realized something, something I hadn't realized before. I said to myself, 'I'm not Val.' It was wonderful. So peaceful. I said, 'I'm not Val. I'm not an old woman. I'm not this and I'm not that. I'm just me. I'm me! And I love it!' And I haven't felt the same since.[9]

Val's experience here is similar to Byron Katie's in the last chapter – a moment of complete clarity and realization, a sudden dis-identifcation with the person she had been before ('Val') and a rebirth as a new person. She had made contact with her true self – what the Indian Upanishads call the *Atman*, the pure spiritual self beneath the superficial identity of the ego.

After this, Val was reconciled to death. She lived nine months longer than expected and spent her final months feeling more whole than ever before: 'I know that I'm dying, piece by piece. There's no denying that. But what's very odd is that I don't feel any less. It's almost like I feel I'm *more* than I was before.'[10]

She had another powerful experience before she died, a vision she interpreted as showing that there was life after death. She saw herself riding a beautiful white horse, and she kept riding until they reached the edge of a precipice:

I went to another level of consciousness... I knew it wasn't a dream, because all the time I knew I was there, and not here, if you see what I mean... There, way, way down [over the precipice], and stretching as far as I could see in all directions, was a city of light. Everything there was made of light. Everything! And I just stood there and stared at it... It was so beautiful. I'd never thought I would see anything like that.[11]

His relationship with Val had an awakening effect on Paul too. It made him re-evaluate his life. He stopped watching TV and his marriage broke up because he didn't feel able to compromise his true self any more. He developed a new spiritual awareness, an ability to sense the connectedness of everything. He now sees death not as a tragic and catastrophic ending, but as 'an opportunity, a fulfilment of all that has gone before'.[12]

OTHER CASES

In his work as a counsellor at a hospital for cancer patients, Kevin Hinchcliffe, whose own transformational experience we looked at in Chapter 5, has witnessed transformations similar to those of Dennis Potter and Val:

With a lot of the people I work with at the hospital, when they are faced with their own mortality, there is a big shift. All the things that they value, such as their house, their car and their holidays, disappear. They realize that these things have no value whatsoever and start talking about their friends, their loved ones, the sunshine and nature. A lot of people fight against the idea of death right till the end, but others become quite serene. Once they know that they're not going to recover, they accept it and you can see a light in their eyes. You can feel the acceptance and tranquillity all around them, as a kind of aura. Then the difficulty isn't so much comforting the patients themselves, but their relatives. They're the ones who are really suffering.

This is similar to what happened to Deborah Hutton, an English health journalist. In November 2004, she found that she had an aggressive form of lung cancer which had already spread from her lungs to her bones and lymph nodes. It seemed incredibly unfair, since she'd given up smoking 23 years before and had always made a big effort to keep fit and eat healthy food. As she wrote, she was 'never ill, never down, a runner of half-marathons, and yoga freak and nutrition nut to boot'.[13] But over the following weeks she found a new kind of serenity. Just two weeks before she died in July 2005, she told an interviewer, 'I feel that each moment is exquisitely precious. I love the rain. I love the clouds, I love the sun. Each day feels like a gift, and of course it is.'[14]

Treya Killam Wilber, wife of the American philosopher Ken, also became intensely aware of the awakening power of death as she was dying of breast cancer. Treya was already a spiritually developed person, having studied Eastern spiritual traditions and practised meditation most of her adult life. But as her cancer reached its terminal stages, her spirituality deepened and intensified. In her journals – quoted in Ken's moving account of their relationship and her death, *Grace and Grit* – she describes her closeness to death as generating a 'deliciously keen knife-edge of awareness ... this satisfyingly one-pointed focus'.[15] She compared it to 'carrying a meditation master around with me at all times' who could at any moment 'unexpectedly give me a sound whack!'[16]

Treya tried various courses of treatment, some of which seemed to offer hope. However, once she accepted that she was going to die, she developed a new serenity and sense of connection:

The growing acceptance of life as it is, with all the sorrow, the pain, the suffering, and the tragedy, has brought me a kind of peace. I find that I feel ever more connected with all beings who suffer, in a really genuine way. I feel a more open sense of compassion... Because I can no longer ignore death, I pay more attention to life.[17]

Similarly, at the age of 33 the English writer Winifred Holtby was told that she had cancer and probably only had two years left to live. She felt devastated and depressed. Although still young, she had led an incredibly active life and was full of ideals and ambitions for the future. She had been a political activist, fighting for women's rights and supporting the British Labour Party. After a six-month trip to South Africa in 1926, she had fought to bring attention to the oppression of the black population there. She had published 11 books in her short life, as well as writing articles for more than 20 different magazines and newspapers. The news of her cancer seemed incredibly cruel, since she had only recently begun to achieve the success she had sought as an author.

She remained bitter and depressed until a sudden mystical experience reconciled her to her death. One day she was out walking near a farmhouse when she saw some lambs gathered around a frozen water trough. She broke the ice for them and then, as her friend Vera Brittain writes:

[She] heard a voice within her saying, 'Having nothing, yet possessing all things.' It was so distinct that she looked round, startled, but she was alone with the lambs on the top of the hill. Suddenly, in a flash, the grief, the bitterness, the sense of frustration disappeared; all desire to possess power and glory for herself vanished away and never came back...

The moment of 'conversion' on the hill of Monks Risborough, she said, with tears in her eyes, was the supreme spiritual experience of her life.[18]

As a result of this experience, Holtby became aware that 'There is nothing anywhere in the world or without that can make us afraid.'[19]

All of the stories we're heard so far in this book are paradoxical in that they all show that pain and suffering can lead to intense joy and liberation. But these stories of the liberating and awakening effect of death are the most paradoxical of all. Death is the thing we fear most. We associate it with misery, decay and bitterness – the end of all our ambitions, of all the success, status or wealth we've built up, of all the things we enjoy doing, parting from the people we love… But these stories make it clear that it is possible to die happily – joyfully, even. Death isn't always an untimely and painful interruption of life – as Paul McDermott points out, it can be a serene and fitting end to our journey. After battling through our life, struggling against stress, worry and disappointment, in the weeks or months before our death we may find peace and fulfilment. The process of dying may bring the contentment that has eluded us all our life. In *Leaves of Grass*, Walt Whitman wrote, 'Has anyone supposed it lucky to be born? I hasten to inform him or her it is just as lucky to die.'[20] This may not be the case for most people – but for some, it certainly is.

8

RETURNING FROM
DEATH

In his book *Awakenings*, the neurologist Oliver Sacks tells the story of people who contracted sleeping sickness during the 'flu epidemic after the First World War. They were catatonic for 40 years until Sacks gave them doses of the drug L-Dopa. This woke them up again, effectively bringing them back from the dead.

Sacks was worried that, after 40 years, his patients would be disoriented or overwhelmed by reality. But most of them reacted in completely the opposite way. They were like young children, fascinated and amazed by the is-ness and strangeness of the world around them. They were in a state of complete presence, with what Sacks describes as 'an eager and ardent attention on the world, a loving and joyous and innocent attention'. They felt at one with themselves and with the world, with 'a great sense of spaciousness, of freedom of being'.[1]

Sacks believed that all of the patients who 'woke up' experienced this to some degree. He recognized it as a primal and natural state, which was at the same time 'the zenith of real being'. One of the patients, Leonard L. (played by Robert de Niro in the film of the book), described his state as 'Very sweet, easy and peaceful. I am grateful for each moment for being itself... I feel so contented, like I'm at home at last after a long, hard journey. Just as warm and peaceful as a cat by the fire.' Sacks notes that this was exactly how Leonard *looked* as well, and illustrates it with a quote from D. H. Lawrence: 'All that matters is to be one with the living God/Like a cat asleep on a chair/at peace, in peace/feeling the presence of the living God.'[2]

Unfortunately this state was only temporary. After a few weeks or months, L-Dopa began to wear off or to trigger psychological problems, and so had to be withdrawn. Most of Sacks' patients returned to a near-catatonic state.

But what would have happened if their wakefulness had continued? Perhaps, you might assume, their child-like vision and contentment would have faded after a while anyway, as the world became familiar to them again and they got caught up in the stress and worries of everyday life. In a similar way, Treya Killam Wilber wondered what would happen if she recovered from cancer. Would she lose her heightened awareness and sense of connection? she asked herself. In some ways, as for Sacks' patients, this is what you might expect. If an awakening such as Treya's was caused by the close proximity of death, then surely if the threat of death were taken away, the experience would fade, in the same way that the intoxication of a beautiful landscape fades once you have left it.

However, we'll see in the next two chapters that there are many cases where this doesn't happen. Like travelling to the moon, and like many of the experiences of intense suffering we've looked at in this book, close encounters with death often bring about a *permanent* psychological shift. If it's lucky to die, then perhaps those who have close encounters with death and then return to life are even luckier.

To an extent, Carrie and Iris are both examples of this – they were both told that they might only have a certain amount of time left to live, but recovered, and were both permanently transformed by the experience. (Although for them the transformation was gradual rather than sudden, and encountering death was only one aspect of their trauma.) In this chapter we're going to look at other examples.

HUGH MARTIN: FROM TERMINAL CANCER TO PERSONAL TRANSFORMATION

Hugh Martin is living proof of the permanent and positive effects of encountering death. His meeting with death happened over 40 years ago, but the awakening he experienced has never faded.

In his mid-twenties, Hugh was a graduate student, spending the summer with his wife and young baby in his aunt's house in Chicago. While his 97-year-old grandfather was dying of old age upstairs, Hugh suddenly fell seriously ill too. His fever rose to 105 degrees and he was too weak to get out of bed. The fever kept rising, and after a week his family realized it must be something more serious than 'flu. When Hugh was taken to hospital for tests, the results were a devastating shock. The biopsy showed Hodgkin's disease, a cancer of the lymph system that had invaded his whole body. The doctors told him it was incurable and he had no more than two years left to live.

Once the initial shock and horror subsided, Hugh decided to make the best of the time he had left. As he describes it now, 'The cancer was a catalyst. It was a flashing warning sign, a blaring wake-up call, telling me not to waste my life – to live for the moment, because our whole life is just a series of precious moments.'

He decided to give up academic life and move to Berkeley, California. There, while under observation for his illness at Stanford University Medical Centre, he was swept up in the whirl of psychological, social and spiritual transformation of the mid-1960s. Although he'd never paid serious attention to self-development before, he now felt impelled to explore different perspectives and different states of consciousness. He moved with his family to Big Sur to become part of the Esalen Institute, the psychological and spiritual growth centre founded under the influence of Alan Watts, Aldous Huxley and Abraham Maslow. There he immersed himself in self-exploration – he learned meditation, experimented with LSD and peyote, explored Gestalt dreamwork and primal Reichian bodywork, and embraced natural and holistic medicine.

In the midst of this self-exploration, a miracle occurred – the cancer which was supposed to be incurable faded away and disappeared. The doctors at Stanford were astonished, and suggested that the original diagnosis might have been wrong. Since then, however, many eminent psychologists and natural medicine practitioners have assured Hugh that the remission was more likely due to the psychological healing he'd experienced and the authentic new life he was leading.

Hugh continued to be observed at Stanford, but the cancer never reappeared; after five years he was officially pronounced 'cured'. However, the psychological and spiritual transformation that came with the cancer has never diminished. As Hugh describes it:

No matter how long the reprieve, I've always lived as
if I have only two years left. Even now, I still sense the

raven of death sitting on my shoulder, reminding me that life is very short and that each day is an amazing gift. The cancer continues to bring me back to the present, makes me feel that I have to live in the now, to focus on what's really important. As a result I always choose to do what gives me the deepest satisfaction, in my activities, my interests, my companions, my occupations. I know that every moment is fleeting, and therefore immeasurably valuable.

I feel that something or someone greater than myself is watching over me, guiding me, giving me another opportunity, a second chance at life. So I try to stay tuned to that higher power. I've been developing psychologically and spiritually ever since. The processes continue to change, but the quest remains.

Most people my age have stopped growing long ago; their minds have become fixed in the same old patterns and they keep repeating the same self-defeating behaviours. But I'm still exploring, still developing. It's remarkable – I keep thinking I've seen it all, but then something new comes along and I'm embarking on a new journey all over again.

Now 70 years old, Hugh is still as active and productive as ever. Over the past three years, he's written six books and created a language arts curriculum for home-schooled children. He also works as a counsellor and regularly goes back-packing and mountain biking to remote areas with his grandchildren. And he's sure that his life would not have been so rich and so fulfilling if it hadn't been for his encounter with death. As he says, 'It's a great blessing to experience first-hand the brevity of life. It teaches you to savour every moment and inspires you to live life at a level you never dreamed possible.'

IRENE

Another person who returned from a close encounter with death and whose life has been transformed as a result is a 52-year-old woman called Irene, who was diagnosed with breast cancer 10 years ago. At the time, she was living a hectic life as an IT manager for a medical company. She was – as she realizes now – a workaholic, constantly travelling around the country, with no real interests or ambitions outside her job. She believes now that there was a feeling of incompleteness inside her, a sense of rootlessness which she was trying to numb by working so hard. She put so much effort into her job that people used to say to her, 'You're trying too hard.'

'I didn't understand what they meant,' she says now. 'I thought, "How can you try too hard?" I strongly believe that your body sends you messages. And if you choose to ignore them it gets to a point where it says, "I'll tell you something that you really can't ignore."' (It's obviously too simplistic to suggest that there may be a connection between overwork and cancer, but it's interesting that Iris, Carrie and Cheryl all described themselves as workaholics and perfectionists too.)

Irene bypassed the phase of bitterness and depression most people experience after being diagnosed and had a transformational experience straightaway:

It was almost instantaneous, overnight. It was the first time I'd seen death as a reality and realized that life was just temporary. The following day I woke up and thought, 'I'm just so lucky to be alive.' Although it was raining, it was just wonderful. The air was so clean and fresh and everything I looked at seemed so vibrant and vivid. The trees were so green and everything was so alive – I was just seeing the energy of things. I became aware of an energy radiating from the trees and had a tremendous feeling of connectedness. It was fantastic. I just felt so fortunate to be alive on this planet, to be able to walk in the rain, under this umbrella.

That feeling was really intense for the first few weeks and it's remained ever since. One of my old friends phoned me when she heard I had cancer and I remember saying to her, 'I just feel so privileged to be on this Earth and to have been given this awareness.' Because it just blew me away, it really did. I used to just sit and think, 'This is amazing, that things could just fall into place so quickly.'

The big thing was this connectedness and a tremendous feeling of love and compassion. I became very, very emotional. I could cry at the drop of a hat. I was really appreciating other people, and what I had – everything around me, friends.

Although she felt euphoric, Irene didn't understand what had happened to her until she started a six-month course at an alternative cancer treatment centre. She told one of the therapists what had happened, and the therapist told her, 'That sounds spiritual.' It was the first time she'd heard the word, but from that point, spirituality was central to her life.

Irene almost died twice during her course of chemotherapy, from a condition called neutropaenia, when the body has very few or no white blood cells. However, she recovered with the help of a visualization technique she created:

> *I imagined myself driving around my village in a little van, collecting these white cells. The next day I had a blood count and they told me, 'Your white cells have increased, but your red cells haven't.'*

> *I said, 'That's because I didn't collect any red ones!'*

Irene responded well to the gruelling treatment regime, which included the removal of her lymph nodes, a mastectomy, chemotherapy and radiotherapy. Despite a poor prognosis, the cancer has never returned. But, as with Hugh Martin, the psychological change she underwent has remained. She still feels a powerful sense of connection and has found a new pleasure in just *being*:

> *I have this inner connectedness with other people, with the whole universe – this sense of how we're all related and that what I do will have an impact on the whole of the web of nature.*

> *I just love being on my own. If I've got a clear day in my diary, it's great. I love to just sit and be. But at the same time I love the new people who've come into my life, the networking aspect of it. Not so much with my husband, because he just thinks I've gone totally crazy, but that's his problem. I feel alive.*

> *It's interesting – you go along with these things that happen throughout life, but you don't actually know why they're happening when you're going forward.*

It's only when you look back that you can join the dots together and say, 'Ah, that's the reason.' It's almost as if getting cancer gave me what was missing from my life, almost as if it was the last piece of the jigsaw, and now I feel whole.

Like many of the people we've heard from, once she was fully recovered Irene didn't feel she could go back to her job. In a similar way to Iris, after neglecting her own self for years, she wanted to focus on her well-being and development. She learned meditation and yoga, studied Buddhist Dharma teachings, trained to be a life coach and has recently studied psychology, counselling and understanding cancer with the Open University. She now runs a lifestyle club at the local hospital for breast cancer patients. But at the same time, she's aware of the importance of *letting* things happen rather than forcing them to:

I know we create our suffering for ourselves, with the thoughts that we think. We have to welcome everything into our lives. We can't be selective and just think 'I want to be happy, I want to do this.' We have to experience the good and bad and realize that everything happens for a reason, for us to learn from.

The journey has just been incredible. When I was working my attitude was, 'I've got to make things happen.' But now it's not trying so hard, it's letting things happen. I think that's been the biggest lesson, because I used to push myself so hard. I was unkind to myself, whereas now I've learned compassion and kindness for myself. I've connected with the authentic me – and that is such a great feeling.

My maxim for life is this quote by Zen-master Suzuki Roshi: 'Knowing life is short – enjoy it day after day, moment after moment.'

D. H. LAWRENCE

It's no coincidence that, in his description of the effects of his patients' awakening, Oliver Sacks quotes from the English author D. H. Lawrence. Lawrence is best known as a novelist, for books such as *Lady Chatterley's Lover* and *Sons and Lovers*, but in my view he should really be seen as a mystic, who lived in a state of permanent wakefulness.[3] Lawrence had an amazingly intense perception of the world, which gave him access to a dimension of beauty, meaning and harmony that is hidden from most of us. Aldous Huxley – another great English novelist, and author of *The Doors of Perception* – was one of Lawrence's closest friends for the last few years of his life and described him as living in 'a different universe from that of common men – a brighter and intenser world'.[4] He was, Huxley says, 'acutely sensitive to the mystery of the world and the mystery was always for him a *numen*, divine'.[5]

Lawrence was permanently aware of the presence of spirit-force – or *Brahman* – in the world, pervading all things. Since he'd been brought up as a Christian, he usually referred to it as God, or – when he described seeing the divine in all things – 'gods'. For example, in his poem, 'Name the Gods!' he writes:

All the time I see the gods:
the man who is mowing the tall white corn, suddenly, as it curves, as it yields, the white wheat,
and sinks down with a swift rustle, and a strange falling flatness,

ah! the gods, the swaying body of God!
ah! the fallen stillness of god.[6]

As I pointed out in *Waking from Sleep*, Lawrence was also awake in the sense that he felt a strong sense of oneness with animals, plants and nature in general. This is one of the reasons why his novels and short stories make such exhilarating reading. He could experience the *being* of other people, and even other creatures, and so describe their experience of the world with amazing vividness. As Huxley put it, 'He seemed to know, by personal experience, what it was like to be a tree or a daisy or a breaking wave or even the mysterious moon itself. He could get inside the skin of an animal and tell you in the most convincing detail how it felt and how, dimly, inhumanly, it thought.'[7] Lawrence himself expressed his one-ness with the world in a more direct way in poems such as 'Mana of the Sea':

And is my body ocean, ocean
whose power runs to the shores along my arms
and breaks in the foamy hands...
I am the Sea! I am the Sea![8]

To some extent, this wakefulness was probably natural to Lawrence. He never practised meditation or yoga and never followed any path of spiritual development. Neither was there any particular point of realization or transformation, when he suddenly woke up. His wakefulness always seems to have been there. However, it's probably also very significant that he spent most of his life with the shadow of death hanging over him.

Lawrence was close to death almost from the moment he was born. He was born into a poor mining community in 1885, when infant mortality rates were still high. He nearly died of bronchitis when he was just two weeks old, and even when he survived that, his mother didn't expect him to live past three months. People who knew him as a child said he was the tiniest and thinnest boy they had ever seen. He was so delicate that he never played sports with other boys and was bullied as a result.

As an adult, he had his first serious brush with death at the age of 26, when he caught pneumonia. He only just survived and was so weak that he was bedridden for two months and only able to sit up after six weeks. He was told by his doctor to give up his job as a schoolteacher, otherwise he would develop tuberculosis. After four months, when he was fully recovered, he felt changed by his illness, more liberated and independent, as if it had, in his words, 'broken a good many of the old bonds that held me'.[9]

Lawrence's next brush with death was in 1919, when he 'nearly shuffled off the mortal coil' (in his words) after catching Spanish 'flu in the epidemic that killed millions of people after the war. Then in 1925, while living in Mexico finishing his novel *The Plumed Serpent*, he caught malaria, typhoid and then pneumonia again, which led to a bronchial haemorrhage. A doctor in Mexico City confirmed what Lawrence must have already known – that he had been suffering from tuberculosis for years and it was now at an advanced stage.

Lawrence had an incredible fire of creativity – despite the poverty and illness (and hostility from his home country) that blighted most of his 44 years, he wrote over 30 books and close to 1,000 poems, as well as many journalistic pieces. (He also painted dozens of paintings.) And even while lying in bed close to death in Mexico, he managed to dictate the first pages of a short story, 'The Flying Fish', to his wife – although he never felt able to complete it, because it had been 'written so near the border-line of death, that I have been unable to carry it through in the cold light of day'.[10]

From this point on, Lawrence was slowly dying, and it was a miracle that he managed to survive for another five years. According to Aldous Huxley, it was only his amazing vitality – the force that produced his constant flow of creativity – that kept him alive 'long after the time, when, by all the rules of medicine, he should have been dead. For the last two years he was like a flame burning on in miraculous disregard of the fact that there was no more fuel to justify its existence.'[11]

However, when Huxley visited Lawrence at his sanatorium in France in spring 1930, it was obvious that he was nearing the end. He was severely emaciated, weighing less than six stone, and had lost his appetite and stopped responding to treatment. Huxley was at his side when he died, on 2 March 1930, after an attack of pleurisy.

This constant closeness to death surely intensified Lawrence's natural wakefulness. As a young man, he must have known – subconsciously, even if he didn't allow himself to think about it – that his life was going to be cut short, and so been aware of the precious temporariness of life and acutely attentive to present-tense reality. And his three close brushes with death must have intensified this awareness, making him acutely sensitive to the beauty and wonder of the world. Perhaps it was his awareness of death that stopped the world becoming mundane or familiar to him and that enabled him to live such a liberated, self-sufficient life, without any attachment to or concern about material wealth, security or success.

Huxley hints at the relationship between Lawrence's intense perception and his awareness of death in the following passage:

He looked at things with the eyes, so it seemed, of a man who had been at the brink of death and to whom, as he emerges from the darkness, the world reveals itself as unfathomably beautiful and mysterious. For Lawrence, existence was one continuous convalescence; it was as though he were newly re-born from a mortal illness every day of his life.[12]

For Lawrence, this wakefulness was a constant, permanent state, even during the times when he wasn't close to death. However, as for Treya Killam Wilber, during the last months of his life his spiritual state deepened. The poems he wrote during this time – published after his death as *Last Poems* – are both the most profound and spiritual works he wrote, filled with an awareness of spiritual radiance pouring through the world, pervading it with harmony and meaning. The poems show Lawrence at times serene and at peace, at one with himself and the world, and at other times wildly ecstatic at the beauty of nature.

The *Last Poems* are also moving for the courage and acceptance with which Lawrence faces his own death. He has no fear of death, because at the high intensity of wakefulness he attained during his final months, there is an awareness that there is really no such thing as death. As a result, like Walt Whitman (who tells a dying friend, 'I do not commiserate with you, I congratulate you'),[13] he saw death as an occasion for rejoicing rather than fear or mourning. Death is a kind of liberation, the beginning of what Lawrence calls 'a great adventure' where we attain the fulfilment that may have eluded us during this lifetime. In death, as he writes in his poem 'Gladness of Death', 'the winds of the afterwards kiss us into the blossom of manhood' and 'after the painful, painful experience of dying there comes an after-gladness, a strange joy'.[14]

SPIRITUAL TRANSFORMATION ON THE BATTLEFIELD

Long-term illness is the most common situation where the threat of death hangs over us constantly, but another is warfare. In a sense, soldiers in a war zone (and victims of war such as civilians living in a war zone or prisoners of war) are in a similar situation to cancer patients, knowing that death could strike them down at any moment. And as a result – absurd though it might sound – there is a possibility that war can bring about spiritual transformation too.

This is what happened to the German spiritual teacher and author Karlfried Graf von Dürckheim, who died at the age of 92 in 1988. Von Dürckheim was from a wealthy aristocratic family and was brought up to be proud and patriotic. When he was 18, the First World War broke out and he felt it was his duty to volunteer as a soldier. After his privileged upbringing, the horrors of the battlefield were a massive shock. He fought for all four years of the war, on several different fronts, including in the nine-month Battle of Verdun, where a quarter of a million soldiers died. He lost count of the number of deaths he witnessed, or the number of times he came close to death himself. However, the close proximity of death triggered a spiritual awakening in him. It made him aware that there was a part of his being that could not die, since it wasn't physical. As he wrote, 'When death was near and I accepted that I also might die, I realized that within myself was something that had nothing whatsoever to do with death.'[15]

This was the beginning of a lifelong spiritual journey for Dürckheim. After the war he renounced his family property and inheritance and began to study Eastern spiritual texts. He had a major spiritual experience while reading the ancient Chinese text the *Tao Te Ching*, when he felt as if 'the veil was torn asunder... Everything existed and nothing existed. Another Reality had broken through this world. I myself existed and did not exist.'[16]

When the Nazis came to power, Dürckheim was sent to Japan as an envoy. There he studied Zen Buddhism for several years, learning Zazen meditation, the Japanese tea ceremony and the Zen approach to archery. (He was later one of the first westerners to introduce Zen teachings to the West.)

When he came back to Europe after the Second World War, Dürckheim became aware that the transformation he'd had in the face of death was by no means uncommon. He came across many examples of people who had lived through the horrors of this new war and had similar experiences. As he later stated:

> There are so many people who went through the battlefields, through the concentration camps, through the bombing raids. And within their hearts they retain the memories of those moments when death was near, when they were wounded and nearly torn in pieces, and they experienced a glimpse of their eternal nature.[17]

He found cases of soldiers who had heard the whistle of a bomb falling straight at them and been certain they were going to die. They had accepted it and suddenly everything made sense – they realized that there really was no death. But the bomb didn't go off and they survived. He found cases of concentration camp inmates who had been there so long that they had lost all hope of ever getting out alive. But somehow, rather than plunging them into despair, accepting this fact had freed them and given them a sense of their own eternal spiritual essence. And finally, he found cases of people who were refugees, hundreds of miles away from home, who had lost everything – their friends and relatives, their jobs, houses, possessions and savings – with no hope of ever getting anything back. But again, once they accepted this fact, they felt a powerful sense of liberation and joy.[18]

Dürckheim explained these effects in terms of surrender and acceptance. In his view, when our resistance to death dissolves away, we become calm and free of fear. The 'hard shell' of the ego breaks down and we make contact with our true spiritual nature, the part of us that is beyond death.[19]

9

SUDDEN ENCOUNTERS
WITH DEATH

From the examples we've seen so far, it's clear that intense encounters with death have a number of common effects. First, they make us aware of the *value* of life. We realize that life is too precious to be wasted and so feel invigorated. We become free of what could be called the 'illusion of permanence', the subconscious assumption that we're *not* going to die. Normally death isn't a reality to us and so we don't live in terms of it. But a close encounter with it wakes us up to our real predicament, making us realize our time is limited, and therefore precious.

One effect of this is to make us re-evaluate our lives. Like Hugh Martin, we question the course our life has been taking and decide to change it in favour of a more productive and meaningful path. We realize that life is too valuable to waste doing jobs that don't fulfil us, or to spend with people who don't truly love us, or we don't truly love. We feel a sense of urgency and become more willing to take risks, knowing that we only have a limited amount of time on our hands.

This can lead to a new sense of purpose too, a desire to put our limited time to good use, to help others or to further our own personal development.

Becoming aware of the brevity and preciousness of life also frees us from what I call the 'taking for granted syndrome' – our tendency not to appreciate things in our lives which we ought to be thankful for, such as our health, the people we love, our peace and freedom, the fact that we don't have to worry about our basic material needs (compared to other people in history or in the world) and the very fact that we're alive at all. We get used to these blessings and don't see our lives in wide enough perspective, in relation to other people who aren't as lucky as us. But, like the astronauts who went to the moon, after encountering death we no longer take life – and all the things in it – for granted. We feel grateful just to be alive, to have been born into this world for a short time. We appreciate the beauty and wonder of nature, like Dennis Potter gazing at the blossom outside his window. We feel a new appreciation for the people in our lives and for mundane everyday things, such as food, water and the weather.

Encounters with death also make us more present-centred. This is partly because we know we may not *have* a future, or at least only a short-term one, and so we stop looking towards it, rushing into it or filling it with goals and ambitions. We realize that the future and past don't really exist, except as ideas in our heads, that life only consists of the present, and that what is precious about life *is* the flowing present we're living through. As Dennis Potter put it, 'The fact is that if you see, in the present tense – boy, can you see it; boy, can you celebrate it.'[1] Or in Hugh Martin's experience, his brush with death 45 years ago 'continues to bring me back to the present, makes me feel that I have to live in the now, to focus on what's really important'. (This present-centredness is also part of the reason why we become more aware of beauty and wonder. It means that we become naturally more *mindful*, more attentive to our present experience, so that our perceptions become de-automatized and we become more sensitive to the raw is-ness and beauty of the world.)

Related to this, encountering death can also quieten the normal chattering of our mind. This is partly because a lot of our mental chatter is *about* the future and the past – thoughts about what we have to do at work next week, about our holiday in a few weeks, about achieving our ambitions, or about what we did last week or further back in the past. But it's also because death gives us a sense of perspective. It makes us aware that a lot of the things we worry about simply aren't important. Normally you might worry about whether other people like you, about not being able to find a perfect partner or about your job – that you're not as good at it as you should be or that you're not taking the right career direction. You might feel guilty that you're not doing enough exercise, not working hard enough, that you haven't contacted certain people for a long time or haven't achieved your ambitions. But in the shadow of death, all of these 'problems' dissolve into insignificance. They're too trivial to waste time thinking about and so our mind stops mulling over them. As a result, the mind becomes quieter than normal. Thought-chatter slows down; we become free of the negative feelings generated by our thoughts, and stiller inside, so that we're able to make contact with the natural well-being inside us.

There's an example of this in Alister Hardy's collection of spiritual experiences, *The Spiritual Nature of Man*, where a man describes how, at the age of 55, he developed all the signs and symptoms of cancer. His doctor told him that no other diagnosis was possible and that he might only have a year left to live. However, rather than feeling devastated, the man felt happier than ever before. For the first time in his life, his mind was free of niggling worries: 'I spent a weekend of deepest happiness. All my worries disappeared ... I truly for once took no anxious thought.'[2]

In the cases we've looked at so far, these changes have occurred as a result of sustained encounters with death – episodes of illness (mostly cancer) which lasted for several months. However, it doesn't always require a long-term encounter with death to bring about spiritual transformation. It can also come from sudden short-term encounters, such as accidents and sudden medical emergencies.

THE JUMPERS

In the summer of 1985, Ken Baldwin decided to commit suicide. He had suffered from depression since his teens, and now, at the age of 28, the stress and sleeplessness of new parenthood had made his condition much worse. There was a voice inside his head telling him that he was a failure, a waste of space. He was convinced his wife and young child would be better off without him. He'd tried to kill himself once before, with an overdose of painkillers, but this time he was determined to succeed. He told his wife he would be back late from work and drove three hours from his home to the Golden Gate Bridge in San Francisco.

The Golden Gate Bridge is the most popular suicide spot in the United States, perhaps even in the world. In the 75 years since its opening, at least 1,300 people have committed suicide there, an average of almost 20 people per year, or one person every 16 days. The bridge is so popular partly because of its beautiful and romantic location, but also because it's such a fail-safe way of dying. Every jumper has a 98 per cent chance of success, a much higher percentage than for hanging, a drugs overdose or shooting. The bridge is 225 feet high, and after a four-second fall, jumpers hit the water at a speed of 75mph, with a force equivalent to a lorry crashing into a wall.

At 10 o'clock in the morning, Ken Baldwin walked calmly onto the bridge and jumped straight over the rail. But as soon as his arms let go, he knew he'd made a mistake. Despite all his years of contemplating suicide, he knew that he didn't want to die after all. As he describes it, 'I thought, "What am I doing? This is the worst thing I could do in my life." I thought of my wife and daughter. I didn't want to die. I wanted to live.' He recalls realizing that 'everything in my life that I'd thought was unfixable was totally fixable – except for having just jumped'.[3]

Luckily, Ken fell feet first into the water, which is the only possible way of surviving. The shattering of the femur bones in the legs can sometimes shield the body's vital organs from the full impact of the fall. With the image of his wife and daughter in his head and his heart full of regret, Ken blacked out. He came to a few minutes later, on the deck of a rescue boat with the coastguard asking him: 'Do you know what you did? Do you want to do it again?'

Even at that moment, he knew that he wasn't going to try to kill himself again. Lying on the boat, he felt thrilled to be alive, to be given another chance. However, for several hours it wasn't clear whether this second chance would materialize. Although he hadn't broken any bones, there was severe bruising to his lungs. He spent the night in intensive care, with only a 50 per cent chance of survival.

But once he recovered, Ken felt an intense gratitude for his life, which has never left him:

*Before, I didn't want to get better. I had become
consumed by my depression. But after the jump, that*

*changed because now I knew I wanted to live... Most
people just have one life that goes from high school to
college to marriage, job and kids. I have two lives: one
before the jump, one after. I'm almost a completely
different person now. I know now that I'm lucky to be
alive. I may have had a crummy day at school [Ken is
now a high-school teacher], but I have my life.*[4]

In other words, his suicide attempt led to a psychological
shift, even a spiritual transformation. And his story is by no
means exceptional.

In 1975, when only 10 people were known to have
survived jumping off the bridge (the figure is now 26), the
psychologist David Rosen sought out and interviewed seven
of them. He found that they had all had spiritual experiences
during or straight after their jumps. They experienced feelings
of intense peace and calm, an awareness of a 'higher power'
and a connection to other human beings or the universe as a
whole. And this state never faded. Although in some cases it
was several years since their jump, they had all retained this
sense of meaning and well-being. In other words, they had
undergone a permanent spiritual transformation.

Most jumpers black out on hitting the water, but two
of Rosen's interviewees had remained conscious and had
profound spiritual experiences right at that moment. As one
of them described it:

*When I hit the water I felt a vacuum feeling and a
compression, like my energy displaced the surface
energy of the water. At first everything was black,
then grey-brown, then light. It opened my mind – like
waking up. It was very restful. When I came up above
the water, I realized I was alive. I felt reborn. I was
treading water and singing – I was happy and it was a*

*joyous occasion. It affirmed my belief [that] there is a
higher spiritual world. I experienced a transcendence
– in that moment I was refilled with new hope and
purpose of being alive.*[5]

This man told Rosen how, ever since his jump, he had been
acutely aware of the preciousness of life and the beauty of
the world:

*It's beyond most people's comprehension. I appreciate
the miracle of life – like watching a bird fly. Everything
is more meaningful when you come close to losing it.
I experienced a feeling of unity with all things and a
newness with all people. After my psychic rebirth I also
feel for everyone's pain.*[6]

Many of the survivors mentioned this new ability to
empathize with other people. They could feel other people's
pain and felt a desire to help them. Perhaps this tells us
something about the nature of depression. Depressed
people are usually self-immersed, so preoccupied with their
own problems that they can't connect with other people's.
Research has shown, for example, that people who suffer
from depression are less likely to respond to requests for
help or charity.[7] But for the jumpers, the fog of their self-
immersion was dissipated by the shock and wonder of their
survival. They became able to reach out beyond their own
egos. One of the jumpers told Rosen that he had 'broken
out of old pathways' and could now 'sense other people's
existence',[8] while another remarked that he now 'loves God
and wants to do things for others'.[9]

As this comment suggests, some of the survivors
interpreted their experiences in religious terms, like Jim Irvin
and Charlie Duke on the moon. One person told Rosen that

before his jump he'd been an agnostic, but in its aftermath, 'I became fully Christian. I believe in God and Jesus Christ. It's still going on. I'm now in a period of painful growth, of being reborn.'[10]

Another survivor used religious terminology, but with a more mystical meaning, saying that since his jump he has felt that there is a 'benevolent God in heaven who permeates all things in the universe' and that all human beings are 'members of the godhead – that great god humanity'.[11]

However, it's probably wrong to think of these transformations as purely the result of a suicide attempt. All of the survivors must have gone through a long period of intense turmoil and trauma before they attempted suicide, which must have prepared them for transformation, as it has for so many shifters in this book. The suicide attempt – and their survival – served as a final release, a moment of surrender and submission which enabled the shift from desolation to liberation to occur.

THE LAUNDERETTE MANAGER

A few years ago a friend of mine told me that I had to go and talk to the manager of a local launderette. 'He's a really spiritual guy,' she told me. 'He's like a guru.' I went there the next time I needed some washing done and as soon as I walked through the door I realized this wasn't an ordinary launderette. There were inspirational quotes from books pinned to the wall, including the Quaker saying, 'I shall pass through this world but once. Any good therefore that I can do or any kindness that I can show to a human being, let me do it now.' And I quickly realized that the tall white-haired man who was busy emptying one of the washing machines wasn't an ordinary launderette manager.

Soon after we started chatting, Tony – as he introduced himself – told me about the dramatic transformation he had been through 15 years earlier, when he'd almost died of a heart attack. Until that time he had been a successful businessman who had devoted his life to making money. He worked up to 60 hours a week, rushing from one appointment to the next and never stopping to think about his life, proving his importance to himself by driving a big car, joining the local golf club and smoking expensive cigars. As he says now, 'I was just going through the motions, not really living.' So when he had a heart attack at the age of 52 it was, he told me, like waking up from a dream:

When I recovered, or even before I recovered, I realized I was like a different person. It may sound ridiculous, but it's the best thing that's ever happened to me. People think I'm mad when I say this, but I think that everybody should have a heart attack that almost kills them, just once and as long as they don't actually die, just to teach them the value of life.

It made me realize that the only important thing in life is not to be successful or wealthy, but to be happy. Living in a big house and having a lot of money in your bank account has got absolutely nothing to do with happiness. Happiness is being aware of how lucky you are to be alive, to be able to see the beauty of the world all around you at every moment. Do you ever stop and tell yourself how wonderful it is just to be able to see? Or how lucky you are to have this healthy body with two arms and two legs? Or how wonderful it is that you've got people around you who love you?

What you should do is get up five minutes earlier than usual every day. And as soon as you get up, go to your window, look at the sky and the trees and the sun and say hello to them all. I mean, really say, 'Hello, trees, hello, sun, hello, sky.' Say hello to every single thing you can see. Remind yourself of how beautiful they are and how lucky you are to be able to see them. And there should be a moment in your day when you just think about all the people you love, all your friends and family, and remind yourself of how special they are and how much they mean to you.

Encountering death has freed Tony from the 'taking for granted syndrome'. He's intensely aware of how lucky he is to be alive, to be healthy and to be surrounded by people who love him. In addition, he no longer takes the *world itself* for granted. In his old life he hardly paid any attention to his surroundings. Even though he lived in a small village in the countryside, he never stopped to look at the beauty all around him. But now, he told me, 'I feel that I'm living in a multi-coloured world compared to a black and white one. Things seem so much more beautiful to me now. The world is an amazingly beautiful place if you look it at properly.' Coming close to death has woken him up to the is-ness of the world and given him a heightened perception of his surroundings. It's also clearly given him a deep inner contentment which he never knew before, a connection to the natural joy at the essence of his being.

Like all of the people we've heard from, once he'd recovered from his heart attack, Tony didn't feel able to go back to his old life. He was no longer interested in his status or in material goods; what was most important to him now was to try to spread the realization he'd had to other people:

I sold my business and bought this launderette so that I could talk to people about what happened to me. I'm here most of the day and I tell people what happened to me and I feel as though I'm making a difference. I love talking to young people especially. They're not aware of any these things – they just take life for granted – so it's interesting to see how they react. Sometimes they think I'm mad, but I still know that something's gone in. As long as I get them thinking, I don't mind. I might be planting a seed in their minds that comes back to them later.

The people at the golf club think I'm mad too. After it happened I sold my Mercedes – it just didn't seem right to drive around in an expensive car any more. Now I just drive around in an old Fiesta. I'm not interested in nice things. I don't want to live in poverty, I want to be comfortable, but I'm not interested in having expensive things just for the sake of it.

In any case, we're all rich, even though we don't realize it. I sometimes say to people who come in here, 'How rich are you?' They usually say, 'I'm not – I'm poor,' or, 'I've got a few hundred pounds.' Then I say to them, 'If I offered to buy one of your legs off you, how much would you take for it? £1,000? £5,000? £10,000?' They might say something like £200,000. So, if you go through your whole body like that, it turns out you're a millionaire. You've got something incredibly precious with you all the time.

I love being by myself, but I love being with other people too. I just love pottering around the house doing nothing in particular. I couldn't have done that before. I would have felt guilty that I wasn't being busy. But I don't have that any more. I'm happy with myself and what I'm doing, even I'm doing nothing in particular.

I know what it means to be alive, how wonderful it is. And I want to share that with as many other people as I can.

Encountering death has also freed Tony from his fear of it. As he says, 'Life is precious. But you shouldn't be afraid of death either. Death is natural. It's a stage, it's not the end.'

NEAR-DEATH EXPERIENCES

One evening in April 1999, a friend of mine, the author and activist William Murtha, was cycling along the path by the sea wall in his home town of Dawlish, Devon. At the time he was working 15-hour days as a sales director for an international company. He had a large salary and lived a hedonistic and materialistic lifestyle – designer suits, big cars, expensive foreign holidays with his family. His life was fast and stressful and he drank and took drugs to keep himself going.

But that evening his life changed. A massive freak wave knocked him off his bike and another, even bigger one swept him into the sea. The current took him away from the sea wall and dragged him further and further out.

Luckily William was very fit – he regularly played sport – and a good swimmer, so he could keep himself afloat, at least initially. He also had the presence of mind to take off his heavy fleece jacket, which would have dragged him down.

As it was dark and the sea wall deserted, nobody had seen him go in, and the roar of the sea was so loud that nobody heard him shouting. He was in the water for nearly two hours, fading in and out of consciousness and suffering from hypothermia. But he had some amazing good fortune:

a man who lived in an apartment close to the seafront happened to be looking through a telescope at the night sky and spotted him in the sea. He alerted one of his neighbours, they threw a buoy out to him and after a 20-minute struggle, William was pulled to safety.

William had been on the verge of death in the water; he believes that he actually did die for a short time. And while he was unconscious – or 'dead' – he had an incredible experience:

I left my body and was out in space, and had the feeling that I was the air, the clouds – I became everything. There was no boundary to my identity. Then, while I was out of my body, I became aware of a higher presence, a being, which radiated an amazing benevolence, a warm-hearted and gentle feeling. This being started communicating with me and I started asking it questions about life. It answered so many questions I'd asked since childhood, such as 'Why we are here?', 'What's our purpose on Earth?' and 'What happens when we die?' The two-way conversation was phenomenal and went on to show me without question how we are all intrinsically linked to the same web of energy.

Then I was given a replay of around ten to a dozen past experiences which I now have defined as probably the most emotionally traumatic times of my life. It was almost as if they were being replayed to make me see them from a higher, alternative perspective.

After his rescue, William felt relieved and grateful to be alive, but found it difficult to accept the content of his near-death experience. Like many of the people we've heard from, he didn't have the framework to understand his experience and so tried to deny it. As he puts it, 'I didn't come from a spiritual background at all. I thought, "How do I frame this? How do I tell people about this?" So I didn't. I acted as if it hadn't happened. I was in so much denial that I actually went back to work a few days after it happened, even though my company was telling me to take a few weeks off.'

He denied the experience for another 18 months. Subconsciously he must have realized that it had destroyed the value system he had been living by, and in response he clung to those values more tightly. He worked even harder, drank even more and took more drugs. But one night during a work trip to Amsterdam, he experienced a sudden shift. The transformation of consciousness he'd been trying to suppress suddenly burst through his resistance:

I was in a café at three o'clock in the morning, talking to some clients. I'd been drinking and taking drugs all weekend. All of a sudden I heard this little voice at the back of my head, saying, 'Bill, this is not who you are, you are not meant to be here.' And I can just remember stopping in my tracks and I sobered up, just like that. All of a sudden I just got it. Everything became crystal clear. I just thought, 'What am I doing? I'm running away from the truth of what happened to me and all the bizarre experiences I went through 18 months ago.' I was running away from it because of my narrow worldview, my conditioning, what I'd learned at school, the scientific model of the Newtonian and reductionist world I'd been taught.

It was like a switch going on. I could feel a shift inside me. You feel it on a vibrational level. It's like a gut, heart knowing. You don't know why you know, but there is a massive gear shift. There's a little gear shift when you see the most stunning red sunset in your life, and when your child is born, and so on, and this was like all of those put together.

Straightaway, William was aware that his worldview and his values had changed. He felt as though he was seeing the world from a wider and deeper perspective:

You start to become more of an observer than a doer. You start to sit back in conversations a bit more. You start to view things a bit more. You start to look for the metaphors in life, the symbolism of what people say and do. It's almost as though you've gone along the surface all your life, believing that that's all there is, and then suddenly someone's come along with this epiphany, and suddenly you realize that there is a whole ocean underneath the surface, that there is a depth and breadth and a profound uniqueness that you never realized was there. And once you start tapping into it you realize that it goes on forever...

There's a rhythm, a life-force – you can call it 'universal spirit', 'life', 'the divine', 'soul', 'God', whatever handle you want to put on it. It's the awareness that there is something else going on under the surface. You know it's profound, you know it's divine, you know it's unique and you know it's powerful, and you know you're swimming along with it, as opposed to just observing it.

Even though we had the BMWs, the holidays to America, the designer suits, a big house – none of it seemed to matter any more. My life seemed too materialistic, too empty.

This psychological transformation deepened William's relationships, too, and gave him a heightened sense of the beauty of the world:

Once you allow this new understanding in, relationships become much deeper, richer, broader. When you see your parents, rather than asking superficial questions, you're really interested in them. You're suddenly like a budding psychologist, much more interested in people and their behaviour. You realize that we're all actually interlinked in some miraculous, wonderful way.

I started to see a more sacred, more profound aspect to the whole of life. I became aware of the colour and beauty and wonder of life. When you go to Paris or New York, or even the top of Dartmoor, you see the most stunning sight and you know that you're never going to see that sight again because it's something beautiful and unique. But with this conscious shift in awareness, you find that you have lots of small moments like that, in the simplest situations. It could happen when you're watching a bee in a flower. You understand that there's a beautiful weaving of life going on, that we're all interconnected, part of a system, an organism...

And once you move on to that stage, you don't feel the need to be entertained, to watch TV or videos, go to restaurants or football matches, or to do daring sports. You feel that you don't always have be doing, that you can just be at peace with yourself. You can start to enjoy the very simple things in life – simple food, simple company, simple conversations that years ago wouldn't have interested you.

A few months after his epiphany, as he refers to it, William sold his share in the company he'd co-founded and downshifted to a slower and simpler lifestyle. Now he is an author, activist and a philanthropist dedicated to change-making projects. (*See Further Information section for his website.*)

What William experienced when he was on the verge of death in the sea was a 'near-death experience', or NDE. While the term is sometimes used to refer to any close brush with death, in its most specific meaning an NDE is when a person actually does die for a short time before returning to life. The experience often occurs in an operating theatre: for anything from a few seconds to a few minutes, the person's body and brain may have no vital signs, no chemical or electrical activity, while surgeons frantically fight to resuscitate them. However, even whilst physically 'dead', the person may feel that they are still conscious and still be aware of themselves and their surroundings.

In a typical NDE, a person leaves their body and travels through a dark tunnel to a place of light. They may meet deceased relatives or strange beings – sometimes beings of light – who talk to them. They may have a 'life review', in which all the events of their life are replayed in a matter of seconds or where just a few highly significant events are played back to them. And, as for William, NDEs are also usually profound *spiritual* experiences. The person feels a deep serenity and well-being, becomes aware of a radiant, benign 'spirit-force' pervading everything and feels a sense of connection or oneness with the universe.

Not everyone experiences all of these phenomena, but most NDEs include at least some of them. (William's included the out-of-body experience, the encounter with beings and the life review.)

NDEs are not *just* experiences, though; they're also points of transformation, when a shift to a different state of being – and a different kind of psyche – occurs. Follow-up studies have shown that almost everybody who has an NDE undergoes a permanent psychological shift. They become less materialistic and more compassionate, more concerned with helping others than fulfilling their own desires and ambitions. They lose their fear of death, become more interested in spirituality and sometimes even develop paranormal abilities. They also report a much greater capacity for joy and a heightened appreciation of beauty. They return to their lives with a new sense of meaning and mission, and this transformation never fades. As one woman who died for a short time after a heart attack told the researcher Margot Grey:

> The things that I felt slowly were a very heightened sense of love, the ability to communicate love, the ability to find joy and pleasure in the most insignificant things about me... I seemed to have a very heightened awareness, I would say almost telepathic abilities.[12]

While another person who had a near-death experience after a heart attack told Grey:

> Since then, everything has been so different. I go out into the sunlight and I can taste the air; the sky is so blue and the trees are much greener; everything is so much more beautiful. My senses are so much sharper. I can even see auras round trees.[13]

In other words, they undergo exactly the same permanent awakening that we've encountered throughout this book.

It's sometimes assumed that this transformation is due to the content of NDEs – e.g. the encounter with the beings of light or deceased relatives and the life review and the sense of well-being and oneness. However, the other experiences we've looked at suggest that at least part of the transformational effect of an NDE is simply the result of encountering death in itself. After all, we've seen that close brushes with death can cause permanent spiritual awakening, even without the typical content of a near-death experience. In NDEs, however, this transformational effect is combined with the spiritual content of the experience, making it all the more powerful. As a consequence, psychological transformation is much more likely to occur after an NDE than after a normal brush with death.

There is no doubt, then, that encountering death can be the equivalent of travelling to outer space. It's the one experience in our life that is most likely to bring about the psychological shift into permanent wakefulness.

But what good does this do us, you might ask. Does it mean that we have to stage our own encounters with death – contract a fatal disease, throw ourselves off a bridge or jump into the sea – to harness its transformational power? Do we have to risk *actually* dying in order to wake up?

In fact, you could say the same about all the different kinds of turmoil and trauma we've looked at in this book. Since we've established that suffering can bring about permanent awakening, does it mean that we have to inflict suffering on ourselves – make ourselves ill, disabled or depressed, or put ourselves through divorce or addiction? Should suffering become a spiritual path?

This would be absurd, of course. But it doesn't mean that the awakening effect of turmoil or trauma or of encountering death has nothing to tell us about spiritual development. On the contrary, if we could understand *why* suffering has these transformational effects, we might be able to harness them through a different route.

However, before we investigate these questions, it's probably a good idea to try to understand the transformation the shifters have undergone more fully, by looking at the different characteristics of the transformation and at how this state is different from the state of being that most people live in.

PART III

THE SHIFTERS

10

A HIGHER STATE
OF BEING

All of the shifters feel as if they've taken on a completely new identity, almost as if they're different people inhabiting the same body. They all feel that this new identity is permanent; indeed, in some cases it has been decades since their shift, with no diminishing of its effects. (For example, Jamie's shift happened 25 years ago, Kevin's 16 years ago, Eckhart's 30 years ago and Russel Williams' 60 years ago.)

Looking at all of them together, one of the most striking things about these transformations is that they all seem to be a shift into what is essentially the *same* state. I've mentioned before that our normal psyche is a kind of 'mould' which our minds have been fixed into, a mould which is structured in a certain way and consists of certain mechanisms. The main feature of this normal psyche is our strong ego, which has strong boundaries and creates a sense of separateness. This ego is so strong and so active – particularly with the constant 'thought-chatter' it generates – that it uses up most of our mental energy. Its energy requirements are so great that there is a 'desensitizing mechanism' in our minds which turns our surroundings and experiences to familiarity so that we don't use up energy through perception. The energy which could be used through perception is 'diverted' to the ego. That's why, in our normal state, the world around us doesn't seem particularly interesting or beautiful and our experiences don't seem particularly stimulating. Children are free of this mechanism, which is why the world is such a fascinating and intensely real place to them. But as adults, we usually only become free of it when we go away to unfamiliar environments or have new experiences – for example, when we go to a new country.

The higher state of being which the people we've heard from have shifted into is a kind of mould too, a different kind of psyche with a different structure and a different way of working. In Chapter 3, Glyn compared it to a caterpillar turning into a butterfly, and this higher kind of psyche seems to be latent in all of us, in the same way that the 'butterfly' state is latent in a caterpillar.

This metaphor isn't strictly accurate, though, because at the same time as being a 'higher' self, this state is also our truest, deepest nature. Our superficial ego self seems to be imposed on top of it, like a layer of ice over a lake in winter. The normal ego is so powerful that it alienates us from our true nature, although we all tap into it from time to time – after meditation, sex or sport, or through contact with nature, when our thought-chatter quietens and the ego becomes weaker.

Another difference is that, so long as they don't die, all butterfly larvae – or caterpillars – transform into butterflies, whereas very few human beings shift into this higher state. The mould of the normal psyche is so strong that, as we've seen throughout this book, it's often only dislodged after a massive amount of stress and turmoil. (Alternatively, it's sometimes transcended after years of spiritual practices such as meditation, mindfulness and service, or by following an established spiritual path such as Buddhism or yoga.)

But exactly how is this 'butterfly' state different from the normal 'caterpillar' state? Exactly how are the shifters different from their previous state or from those of us who haven't been through this transformation? Here I will summarize what I believe to be the main characteristics of this higher state.

A State of Greater Well-being

All of the shifters remarked on how contented they feel. They all live in a state of natural ease and well-being. They're free of the normal anxieties and worries that afflict most of us. They don't feel the kind of inner dissatisfaction that makes people hanker after more status or success or possessions. They feel happy just to *be*, to exist in the world and in the present moment.

Appreciation

Part of the reason for this well-being is the appreciation the shifters feel. They have all been freed from the 'taking for granted syndrome'. They don't need to 'count their blessings' because they're constantly aware of them. They appreciate how lucky they are to be able to perceive the beauty and wonder of the world, and even to talk, walk, eat and drink – like Gill Hicks, who described how she savours every mouthful of water and every morsel of food. As Tony put it, 'Happiness is being aware of how lucky you are to be alive.'

We all become aware of our blessings sometimes, usually after they've been taken away from us (or at least have been under threat). We become aware of the value of our health after being ill, we appreciate our partners fully after we've been separated from them for a while and we become aware of the value of our freedom after being imprisoned or spending time in a country with an oppressive government. The same thing happens to a less intense degree when we see or hear about people who have serious illnesses, or when we see television news reports about people dying of starvation in another part of the world, and so on. But usually this fades away quite quickly. After a few days or weeks (if we're lucky), we re-adapt to our situation and start taking our blessings for granted again.

However, the shifters have never switched back to 'taking for granted-ness'. Ever since their transformation, they have remained in a state of appreciation and gratitude for everything in their lives, and for life itself.

Intensified Perception

Everyone I have spoken to feels that they have become more aware of the beauty and wonder of the world around them. They have developed the kind of fresh, intense perception of young children, making the world seem more real and alive – and even wonderful and miraculous – to them. The desensitizing mechanism I described above no longer seems to function for them. As Michael – who, if you remember, is paralysed after falling from a bridge while running – describes it, 'Everything I look at has this beautiful and uncanny clarity.' This is why the shifters frequently talk about nature. Whereas before they may not have paid much attention to it, now the natural world is a powerful presence in their lives. They love to spend time contemplating its beauty. As Stephanie said, 'Sometimes I just like to sit there and look at the sky and the trees and my garden, and it's all so beautiful and alive.'

Most of all, it's the 'small things' which become more fascinating and beautiful. As Eckhart Tolle told me of his transformation, 'There was a great sense of appreciation for the little things – not just the spectacular beauty of a flowering tree, but the beauty of even the most insignificant objects, even inanimate objects.'

A Sense of Connection

Almost everyone I spoke to described a powerful sense of connection. The shifters no longer feel a sense of separateness. Rather than being isolated egos looking out at a world 'out there', they are a part of a wider and greater reality, connected to something bigger than themselves. Irene described it as 'this tremendous feeling of connectedness', while Kevin spoke of 'knowing that you are a part of something far more wonderful, far more mysterious'.

This is another reason why the shifters appreciate nature so much – because they feel connected to it. They can sense that the natural world is an interrelated whole, and that they are a part of the whole. As Janice puts it, 'It's not so much a question of appreciating nature as feeling more connected to it and realizing that I need it.'

The shifters also feel a strong sense of connection to other people. Michael is constantly aware of what he calls 'the oneness' – for him, the whole world is pervaded with spirit-force or *Brahman*. And he can always feel this unity between himself and others. 'People can sense that I feel one with them,' he said. Similarly, Irene has an 'inner connectedness with other people, with the whole universe, this sense of how we're all related'.

Better Relationships

Several of the shifters have mentioned that their relationships have become deeper, more fulfilling and more authentic. They now have greater empathy and compassion, a greater capacity to sense other people's feelings and respond to them. As Michael put it, '[Other people] can sense my compassion, and as a result my relationships are much better than they were before.' Janice mentioned that a friend of hers had been diagnosed with cancer and that her friends were trying to avoid the subject, while she felt a strong desire to go and talk to the man. Cheryl told me that she no longer judges or criticizes people – even if they behave egotistically or selfishly, she responds with compassion.

Often when we're with other people – particularly people we see a lot and take for granted, such as partners and close relatives – we don't give them our full attention or listen to them properly. But shifters are more likely to be wholly present and attentive. Carrie recognizes that this is why her relationships have improved after her diagnosis of cancer: 'Because I'm more present with other people, I'm connecting with them more. They've responded to the change in me and become more present as well. So my relationships have definitely improved.' Similarly, William mentioned that when he sees his parents now, he no longer just asks them superficial questions, but is genuinely interested in them.

Incomprehension

However, these positive effects are sometimes offset by a sense of confusion. At first, most shifters don't understand what's happened to them. Like Eckhart Tolle, they know they feel liberated and happy, but don't know why. In most cases, they know little or nothing about spirituality or psychology, and so don't have a framework to enable them to understand what's happened. They try to talk about it to friends, but usually only meet with incomprehension, so that sometimes they start to think that there's something wrong with them, even that they've gone slightly mad (as happened to Russel Williams, for example).

This can last for anything from a few months to a few years. Gradually, though, the shifters are drawn towards books about spirituality, or to spiritual practices like meditation or yoga, or to other spiritually developed people. In every case I'm aware of, they eventually transcend this confusion and establish a conceptual framework which allows them to accept their transformation and integrate it into their lives.

Generally, though, the incomprehension from their friends and relatives continues. This is one of the few negative effects that the shifters have experienced: although they have better relationships with people in general, their relationships with their partners and other close relatives and friends often deteriorate. They have changed dramatically, but their husbands and wives and other relatives and close friends have remained the same, and so a gulf has opened up between them. Many of the shifters commented on this. Irene's husband now 'thinks I've gone totally crazy – but that's his problem', while Tony mentioned that his old friends at the golf club thought he was mad. Iris explained that her mother and son thought she was being selfish for giving priority to her own development – her mother told her, 'I want my old daughter back!'

Quiet Minds

One of the most striking characteristics of the shifters is that thought-chatter seems to have disappeared from their minds, or at least become much quieter. Both Russel Williams and Eckhart Tolle mentioned this. Decades after their transformations, their minds are still quiet. Russel says that he only thinks when he needs to – when he needs to work things out, or to make decisions or plans. For both him and Eckhart, thinking has become voluntary and conscious, rather than automatic.

Stephanie described this very graphically:

The most profound change has been the disappearance of egoic consciousness. There's no little voice in my head. I don't have the ego's constant prompting and fixation on regret and fear. Thinking is not something I do very much any more. This is the most remarkable side effect of the transformation – the lack of internal noise ... and judgement.

For others, the 'little voice' has not stopped altogether, but certainly become quieter and less powerful. For example, Glyn told me that her mental voice still chattered away, but 'I don't feel as involved with it as I used to, and it's getting easier to stop it.'

Pleasure in Doing Nothing and Being Alone

In our normal state, we find it difficult to do nothing or to be alone. Inactivity and solitude make us feel uneasy and so we try to avoid them. But the shifters have a very different attitude: they *relish* inactivity and solitude. They love to be free from activity and distraction so that they can give their attention to the beauty and is-ness of their surroundings, or to the sense of well-being inside them. They have shifted into a mode of 'being' rather than 'doing'.

As Iris put it, 'The old me tried to avoid being by myself – although I hardly ever got the chance anyway – but now I'm quite happy to do nothing on my own.' Similarly, Michael remarked that, 'I love doing nothing. In the summer I can just sit in a reclining chair on my front porch and watch the leaves on the trees, the birds, an ant crawling up my leg. I just disappear.'

Living in the Present

Another characteristic of our normal state is that we don't usually live in the present. Obviously, our body is always in the present, but our mind is often busy with thoughts about the future and the past. Rather than giving our attention to the experiences we're having now, we recall past experiences or anticipate future ones.

In contrast, the shifters have become very 'present-centred'. As Carrie told me, 'Now I live very much in the present. When you have a realization of what really matters, it stops you getting lost in negative thoughts, which I used to do... If I'm with friends and I catch myself thinking about something else, I can bring myself back to the present. Before, I'd just follow my thoughts.'

Similarly, Stephanie told me, 'I pretty much live in the present moment now,' while Glyn described how 'I spend a lot of time in the present. In the past, when friends came round and told me about their problems, I'd get really involved.' (As I mentioned at the beginning of the last chapter, this ability to live in the present is especially strong for people who are – or have been – close to death. Death blots out the future and makes every remaining moment of our life precious.)

And another consequence of this present-ness is that, as Carrie mentions above, the shifters are more present to other people, which creates more authentic and deeper relationships.

Less Interest in Materialism – More Interest in Spirituality

Almost all the shifters said that they were no longer interested – or at least less interested – in making money or acquiring possessions. As Jamie put it, 'I'm not interested in buying things or trying to impress other people.' Or as Glyn said, 'I used to like home comforts, but now I hate having things I don't need. I feel more inclined to give things away. I have no need for them.'

In a similar way, they've become less ambitious, particularly in their careers. Carrie told me that, as a television writer, she used to daydream about winning awards, but now, 'I don't want to win an award for anything. I'm interested in living as harmonious and peaceful a life as possible.'

In this way, the shifters have left the mode of 'having' as well as that of 'doing' – and again, they have swapped this for the mode of 'being'. Rather than attaining wealth or success, what's important to them now is to further their own personal and spiritual development. It's striking how, after having no interest in spirituality before, so many of them have gravitated towards spiritual teachings and traditions and begun to practise meditation. This is partly to enable them to understand what's happened to them, but also because they've discovered a new dimension of their being. After living outside themselves for so long, keeping their minds occupied with activity and distraction, they've discovered their *inner* being.

For most of us, the discord of the ego-mind is a barrier which stops us exploring our own being. We shy away from the discord and keep our attention focused outside ourselves. But for the shifters, the discord of the ego has faded away, enabling them to make contact with the deeper levels of themselves. And they've turned towards spiritual practices and paths to help them explore these deeper levels.

Less Self-centred/More Altruistic

The other main motivation of the shifters' lives, besides furthering their own development, is to help other people. Now that that they feel more connected to others – and are less interested in material things or success or careers – they've shifted away from trying to satisfy their own desires in favour of trying to aid the development and reduce the suffering of others.

Irene – who almost died after being diagnosed with cancer – told me that now she feels she is 'here to help other people who've been diagnosed with cancer'. Kevin gave up his career as an architect to help others through counselling, while Gill Hicks gave up her career in design to campaign for peace and work for charities.

In fact, this desire to do something more altruistic and meaningful (together with their less materialistic and success-oriented attitude) has prompted almost all of the shifters to change their careers. Irene gave up her job as an IT manager and now works as a therapist for breast cancer patients, Tony gave up his business career to become the manager of a launderette and William Murtha gave up his high-flying career as a sales executive.

Stepping Back

Another, more subtle change which many of the shifters mentioned was that nowadays they no longer strive so hard to make things happen in their lives. They no longer feel the need to *push*. Kevin described this as a shift from trying to *direct* life to learning to *follow* it. Or as Irene put it, 'When I was working, my attitude was "I've got to make things happen." But now it's not trying so hard, it's letting things happen.' When Michael discovered this, he felt a massive sense of liberation: 'I was totally free. Everything I did was God's will ... I breathed freely and easily and deeply and effortlessly. *Everything* happened effortlessly.'

As a result of this, the shifters are free of the kind of impatience and frustration most of us feel when events don't unfold as we desire. As Berta put it, 'Before I found it difficult to wait for things to happen, but now I enjoy the waiting. In fact it doesn't bother me much whether things happen or not.'

Rather than trying to make things happen, the shifters have a fundamental trust in life. They feel instinctively that, if they allow it to, everything will work out well for them.

Transcending Fear of Death

Finally, many of the shifters who encountered death mentioned that they were no longer afraid of it, or at least not as afraid as before. Michael described how his encounter with death 'took all fear of death away,' while Gill Hicks wrote that, 'I don't fear death, although I wouldn't choose it.'[1] Similarly, Tony remarked that 'Life is precious. But you shouldn't be afraid of death either.'

This might seem another paradox – after all, most of us are afraid of death and try to avoid thinking about it. And often when we do glimpse our mortality – when people we know die, or when we witness fatal accidents or have health scares – it fills us with anxiety and dread. However, it seems that if we have an *intense* encounter with death (particularly if we do actually die for a short time, as Michael and Gill did) then this fear fades away.

THE CAUSES OF THESE CHARACTERISTICS

All of these characteristics are the result of the shifters' new kind of psyche. The main difference between this psyche and our normal one is that the ego is much less powerful as a structure. It doesn't have a strong boundary, which is why the shifters feel a sense of connection and a strong desire to help others. Rather than being islands of individuality, their identity merges into a collective ocean of being, so that it spreads into all other living things and into the cosmos as a whole.

Because of this softer ego boundary and this sense of connection, the shifters don't have a sense of lack or incompleteness. This is the reason why they are no longer materialistic or success-oriented. In our normal state, our sense of lack creates a desire for material goods and wealth and power. Because our ego is so strong and separate, we feel incomplete and unfulfilled, and seek material goods and success both to try to compensate for our discontent and to try to complete ourselves. And so without this sense of lack, there is no need for wealth or status.

Now that the ego is less powerful, its thought-chatter becomes much quieter. And even when it's there, the shifters don't identify with it. Their identity isn't bound up with the ego any more, but with the deeper self beneath it, so that they're aware that this 'thinking' is really just an automatic mechanism which they don't have to pay attention to or be affected by.

And since the ego is less powerful and less active, it doesn't use up as much energy. This is important because it means that the desensitizing mechanism doesn't need to function. It doesn't need to turn the world to familiarity to save energy for the ego. And this is why the shifters have a heightened perception and see the world as so beautiful and fascinating. They don't perceive the world automatically, but always with fresh, intense perception.

This is also why the shifters live in a state of appreciation. As well as working on perception of the world around us, the desensitizing mechanism works on our life situations. In other words, it's responsible for the 'taking for granted syndrome', switching off our attention to the value of our health, our body, our relatives and friends, our freedom and our very life itself. We 'get used to' these things in the same way that we become desensitized to the reality of our surroundings. But, again because of their less powerful egos, the shifters don't need to save mental energy by having their attention 'switched off' to the reality of their life situations.

The shifters' ability to live in the present is related to their lack of thought-chatter too. As already noted, a large proportion of our thought-chatter is *about* the past and the future – thoughts about what happened to us yesterday or last week, or about what we'd like to happen in the future. So when the thought-chatter stops, we return to the present.

Another reason for their present-ness is that the shifters are no longer so concerned with their future ambitions and achievements, and so are less inclined to turn their attention away from the here and now.

The shifters' state of well-being has a number of different sources. One of them is, again, related to their quiet minds. Our thought-chatter often consists of worries and anxieties – almost always connected to the future and the past – which trigger negative feelings. With their quieter minds, the shifters are less afflicted by this. Their sense of connection means that they're free from another source of anxiety too: our normal basic sense of aloneness, or 'ego-isolation', created by the ego's separateness.

Their lack of (or at least reduced) fear of death obviously enhances their well-being too. At a subconscious level, the fear of death is always there, creating a fundamental anxiety and insecurity. But as Michael puts it, 'Once you've lost your fear of death, your life changes in virtually every way. Fear and anxiety no longer exist in your life.'

At the same time as being free of these sources of *un*happiness, the shifters are in touch with a source of happiness which isn't normally accessible to us: the natural well-being of our true nature. They've become grounded at a deeper level of self, the source of consciousness and energy inside us that we're normally alienated from by our strong egos. This energy has a natural quality of well-being in the same way that sugar has a natural quality of sweetness. We sometimes tap into it in meditation, or at other times when our minds become quiet, but the shifters are permanently in contact with it.

And it's because of this inner contentment that the shifters are able to enjoy doing nothing and being alone. They're free from the fundamental restlessness that normally plagues the human mind, making it difficult for us to be inactive or alone. We need to keep busy and to be in the company of others partly to keep our attention focused outside ourselves, so that we don't give our attention to the discord inside us. But since the shifters no longer have this inner discord, there's no need for them to use activity and distraction as a way of escaping from themselves.

The shifters' ability to 'step back' rather than direct the course of their lives is partly related to their contentment too, and to their sense of completeness. Since they have a sense of well-being and wholeness, they no longer need to strive for more than they have, or to become more important and successful. They're happy with their lives as they are, and so don't feel a strong need to change them. And of course, their weaker sense of ego means that they don't have such a strong urge to assert their identity either, by controlling the events of their own lives or what happens in the world around them. They are content to participate rather than dominate.

Finally, there are perhaps two reasons why the shifters have lost their fear of death. First of all, now that their egos are less powerful and they're less concerned with achievement and ambitions, the prospect of the end of their own individual existence no longer seems as tragic and terrible to them. When your own ego is the whole focus of your life, when you have a strong sense of your past achievements and your future is filled with hopes and ambitions, the end of your life seems a cataclysmic event. It literally *is* the end of the world. But if you don't have such a strong sense of self-importance and feel that you're part of something greater than yourself – something which will continue even if your own individual self dies – then death no longer seems as terrible. In other words, a sense of connection reduces fear of death. Carrie described this very well, saying that she felt 'a lot less encumbered by anxiety and fear of death. When I was diagnosed I was terrified of death. I don't think I'm completely free of it, but I feel much more connected to a wider whole, as an ongoing process of life and rebirth, so the fear has almost gone.'

Perhaps most importantly, though, the shifters have lost or reduced this fear because they have realized that – or at least developed a sense that – death is *not* the end. William, Michael and Gill actually experienced this. They each felt that they did die for a short space of time and continued to be conscious while they were 'dead'. And the 'death' they experienced was certainly nothing to be afraid of – on the contrary, it was a liberating and blissful experience.

Other shifters didn't have NDEs, but were certain from their spiritual experiences that life continues beyond the body. Val was certain of this after her vision of a 'city of light', while D. H. Lawrence's spiritual awareness enabled him to view death as 'a great adventure' in which we would attain fulfilment and peace. Similarly, Glyn is now aware that 'There is only love; there's no real pain or suffering or death. It's impossible… Time only exists inside our cocoon.'

SELF-ACTUALIZATION OR ENLIGHTENMENT?

In the view of the American psychologist Abraham Maslow, the ultimate aim of human life is to attain 'self-actualization'. This is the point where we fulfil our highest potential and become completely integrated and free of inner discord. According to Maslow, 'self-actualized people' are different from others in a number of significant ways. They are wholly positive, free of negative thoughts or feelings, and live spontaneously and freely, without any prejudice towards others. They are less materialistic and self-centred, but more altruistic than other people, with a greater need for peace and solitude and a sense of duty or mission which transcends their personal ambitions or desires. They also have a great capacity for appreciation and a constant freshness of perception. In Maslow's own words, they:

> ...have the wonderful capacity to appreciate again and again, freshly and naively, the basic goods of life, with awe, pleasure, wonder and even ecstasy, however stale these experiences may have become to others... Thus, for such a person, any sunset may be as beautiful as the first one, any flower may be of breathtaking loveliness, ever after a million flowers have been seen... A man remains convinced of his luck in marriage 30 years after his marriage and is as surprised by his wife's beauty when she is 60 as he was 40 years ago.[2]

Strangely, Maslow didn't offer many examples of 'self-actualized' people – he only suggested famous historical figures like Abraham Lincoln, Thomas Jefferson, Albert Einstein and Aldous Huxley. It's difficult to understand why he didn't find examples closer to home, though, because his description obviously fits very closely with the shifters. It seems that they have become 'self-actualized', according to Maslow's definition of the term. Rather than destroying them, the turmoil and trauma they have been through have shifted them into a state of self-actualization.

But even more strikingly, another way of interpreting this state is to see it as one of permanent spiritual awakening.

In *Waking from Sleep*, I showed that spiritual experiences – or higher states of consciousness – have a number of different characteristics. These include an intensity of perception, an awareness of an atmosphere of harmony and meaning pervading the world, a sense of connection or even oneness with the world, love and compassion for other human beings, a sense of inner peace and well-being, and so on. All of the shifters experience these characteristics – the only difference is that for them they are *permanent*. They don't just have temporary spiritual experiences – they live in a permanent spiritual state.

This is the state of 'enlightenment' which spiritual seekers have sought throughout history, the end point of spiritual paths such as Patanjali's eight-limbed path of yoga and the eightfold path of Buddhism, the end point of the lives of renunciation and detachment of monks and hermits. And this state has been reached by completely ordinary people – businessmen and IT managers, architects and TV writers – in most cases, people with no knowledge of spirituality at all. They didn't spend years meditating or reading spiritual texts or learning esoteric rituals – enlightenment just happened to them, against their will, in reaction to their suffering.

Of course, this doesn't mean that all the shifters have become enlightened in the same way that great spiritual teachers like the Buddha, Meister Eckhart or Ramana Maharshi were. As I mentioned earlier, just as there are different intensities of awakening experiences, so there are different degrees of permanent spiritual awakening. All the shifters are in a state of wakefulness, but at varying levels.

Even within the mould of our normal psyche, there are people who experience its characteristics more strongly. There are some whose egos are stronger than others', and who therefore experience more separation and are less capable of empathy. There are people whose vision of the world seems to be more automatic than others, whose thought-chatter is louder and more incessant, or who are more discontented or neurotic.

Similarly, within the mould of the 'awakened' psyche, there are people who experience its characteristics more strongly – people who have a stronger sense of spirit-force pervading the world, a greater sense of oneness with the cosmos, a quieter mind, a stronger sense of well-being, and so on.

However, in my view, there are some shifters who have reached the higher levels of wakefulness or enlightenment – for example, Stephanie, Glyn, Michael Hutchison and, of course, the spiritual teachers Russel Williams and Eckhart Tolle.

SITES AND RELIGIOUS CONVERSION

It may have occurred to you already that, in some ways, SITEs are similar to religious conversions. When a person converts to a religion like Christianity or Islam – or to a cult religion like scientology or the Moonies – they also feel that they're reborn, with a new sense of identity and a new way of seeing the world (hence the term 'born again' Christians). The world suddenly makes sense to them and they feel a new sense of purpose and meaning. Research has shown that religious conversions are often triggered by turmoil and trauma too, especially intense frustration and dissatisfaction and relationship problems. In the *Varieties of Religious Experience*, William James describes conversion as a process by which an individual who felt themselves to be 'wrong, inferior and unhappy becomes unified and consciously right, superior and happy'.[3]

However, there are some major differences between permanent spiritual awakening and religious conversion. For example, whereas SITEs are usually sudden and dramatic, conversions are often gradual. People don't just suddenly convert to Christianity or Islam; it usually happens after a process of 'testing the water', of investigating the religion's beliefs, attending meetings or reading literature. If a person feels that they can accept the beliefs, then there's usually a point when they subconsciously 'allow' themselves to be converted.

Another difference is that conversions mostly happen during adolescence (usually to adolescent males). The typical 'profile' for conversion is a young man who is struggling to find his identity and his direction in life. He feels that he doesn't fit in anywhere, finds it difficult to form relationships and feels confused and depressed. However, most of the shifters we've heard from were women. And on average, they – including the men – were much older when they underwent transformation. The youngest was Hugh Martin, in his early twenties; the next youngest were Russel Williams and Eckhart Tolle, who were both 29. All of the others were in their mid- to late thirties or forties.

More significantly, conversion usually means accepting a set of concepts and beliefs. If you become a Christian you accept the belief system of Christianity and interpret the world in those terms. You believe that Jesus died for your sins and that one day he's going to return to the Earth and take you to heaven. However, permanent spiritual awakening doesn't involve any beliefs. It's not a shift in *belief*, but a shift in *being* and in experiencing the world. If anything, the mind becomes more free of beliefs and concepts. The world is no longer interpreted through the filter of concepts, but in a much more direct and immediate way.

And finally, religious conversion seems to be less stable and permanent than SITEs. Whereas SITEs don't seem to fade, even after decades, conversions are often just temporary. They may be stable for a few years, but eventually the convert's initial fervour begins to fade away. Their sense of alienation and frustration might diminish as they get older, so that they no longer need the psychological support of the religion, or they might convert to another religion of cult, replacing one belief system with another.

Religious conversions are obviously a kind of psychological shift, but a different type. As the psychologists William Miller and Janet C'de Baca write, 'Although they overlap, quantum change [their term for spiritual transformation] is a much larger phenomenon than religious conversion.'[4]

Ultimately, the difference is that with religious conversion, the ego doesn't dissolve away – it simply changes its contents. It's given a new set of beliefs and concepts to support it, which change the way the person interprets the world but not their state of being. The ego is still intact and still as strong and separate as a structure. The convert doesn't lose their individual identity – it's just subsumed into the identity of a group. In fact, this is one of the appeals of conversion – you become part of a something greater than yourself and so feel a sense of belonging and community. But this isn't a transcendence of the ego – in fact, it's a more intense kind of egotism, since at the same time as existing as a separate ego, you're also part of a larger group ego.

The philosopher Ken Wilber makes a distinction between 'translation' and 'transformation'. As he sees it, the main function of religion is to provide consolation and meaning to the isolated ego, to give it hope for the future – especially for the afterlife – and a sense of belonging. But the function of real spirituality is different from this: to provide transformation, to transcend the separate self and enable a new, higher self to be born.[5] In these terms, conversion is usually a kind of 'translation'.

When you undergo a real spiritual shift, you don't feel that you *have* the truth, that your beliefs are the right ones and everyone else's are wrong. Your knowledge stems from your experience, not from belief. You know that life is meaningful, that the universe is a harmonious and benevolent place and that all things are essentially one – *not* because that's the belief system of your religion, but because that's what you *perceive*. With a real spiritual shift, you don't feel a sense of belonging just to your religion or cult, but to the whole human race. You don't feel a sense of oneness just with your God or the other members of your religion, but with the whole cosmos. And you don't need to look to the future for salvation and fulfilment, because you have them right now.

A STATE OF SELF-DELUSION?

When the French novelist Romain Rolland questioned Sigmund Freud about the spiritual experience of becoming one with the universe, the great psychologist explained it (away) as a regression to early childhood, when the infant has yet to develop a sense of individuality and so feels one with its mother. If Freud had turned his attention to SITEs, he might have explained them in a similar way – perhaps as a retreat from a traumatic adult reality into a state of infantile self-delusion.

A couple of sceptical colleagues of mine have suggested something similar – that this 'transformation' is a really just a kind of defence mechanism. In their view, the shifters can't deal with the turmoil and trauma facing them and so switch to a deluded state in which everything is the polar opposite to the harsh reality – where there are no worries or problems, where the world is a benevolent rather than a hostile place and everything is connected rather than separate. This is similar to how 'dissociative personality disorder' (or multiple personality syndrome) develops – in that case, the personality reacts to stress by splitting up, whereas in this case, it reacts by creating a different reality.

The main argument against this view is that the butterfly state that the shifters experience is manifestly not a regression but a *progression*. In every respect, the shifters' state is more integrated and advanced than the normal human state. The shifters have a more intense awareness of their surroundings because they're free of the desensitizing mechanism. They're free (or at least freer) of the psychological discord that plagues the human mind: the constant niggling thought-chatter and the constant sense of discontent and anxiety. They are less selfish, more altruistic and empathic, and have better relationships. Life for them is richer and more fulfilling. Surely a state of regression or delusion would bring an impairment of some form, a loss of ability and a deterioration of function. But in every way, the shifters have gained and improved.

In other words, their state isn't a step backwards to a lower state of development but a massive leap forward. It's not an evasion of reality but a journey *deeper into* reality.

11

THE POWER OF
DETACHMENT

So *why* do trauma and turmoil have this amazing power to dissolve the mould of the normal psyche and shift people into a state of enlightenment? Why do intense stress, depression, disability and illness or encounters with death have the power to dissolve our normal identity and replace it with a higher state of being? How can such intensely negative experiences give rise to something so powerfully positive?

There seem to be two reasons for this, which normally work together. The first – and less important – reason is that when stress or anxiety are constant over a long period and build up to a high enough intensity, they can cause the normal structure of the psyche to dissolve away. The pressure becomes so intense that the structure can't maintain itself. The stress or anxiety is like the tremor of an earthquake which causes the building of the ego to collapse. In most cases, this equates with a 'psychotic break' (or nervous breakdown) – the collapse of the psyche leaves a vacuum and the person feels defenceless and emotionally unstable, unable to cope. But for a few people, this isn't a breakdown but a break-*up* – a new self emerges and fills the vacuum. The 'butterfly self' breaks free and becomes our normal self.

This was probably the main factor in Janice's transformation – after her husband's stroke, she had to care for him at the same time as looking after her children and working full-time. She found it impossible to cope and the stress was so great that, one day when she was walking on the beach, her normal psyche suddenly dissolved away. Similarly, Berta was in a state of intense anxiety for months after being diagnosed with MS, terrified at the prospect of losing her health and mobility.

Stress and anxiety seem to have been the main factors in Russel Williams' and Eckhart Tolle's transformations too. Russel went through a massive amount of stress because of his parents' deaths and his wartime experiences, coupled with a great sense of frustration and anxiety at being out of contact with his true self and not being who he was supposed to be. Eventually, as he describes it, 'The frustration was so great that my old self had to give way.' Similarly, Eckhart suffered from constant anxiety and depression for years, until they intensified to the point that his normal psyche had to give way, bringing about what he describes as 'a death of the sense of self which lived through identifications'.[1]

In fact, this is probably a contributory factor in all SITEs. After all, practically all the shifters went through periods of intense stress and anxiety before their transformations. However, I believe that the *main* reason why suffering can lead to spiritual awakening is because it can bring about a state of *detachment*.

In order to understand this state, we first need to look at its opposite, the state of attachment.

Because our ego is so powerful and separate and feels a basic sense of insignificance and incompleteness, we feel a strong impulse to *add* things to it. As I mentioned in the last chapter, one way in which this manifests itself is the desire for wealth, and for status, success or power. Another way is the impulse to *attach* ourselves to external things. We grasp at external things to try to strengthen the ego, to bolster its fragile structure.

This process starts in our mid-teens, when we first begin to feel the separateness and incompleteness of the ego. That's when we first begin to feel the need to 'belong', or to fit in. Because we feel incomplete, we need to attach ourselves to groups or gangs, to start following fashions or to attach ourselves to pop groups or football clubs by becoming their fans. And as we become adults we gain more and more attachments. We become attached to ambitions for the future (for example, the hope that we're going to be a successful businessman or a famous pop star), beliefs about life and the world (for example, a religious belief system or political beliefs), to the knowledge we've gained, to our past achievements and to our image of ourselves as successful or attractive, and so on.

At the same time, there are more tangible attachments such as our possessions, jobs and careers, and our roles as mothers, fathers, husbands or wives. And of course, there are the people we're attached to – the people on whom we depend for approval and attention, and without whom we feel insignificant or lost.

What about people we are attached to because we love them? you might ask. But real love exists without attachment. Attachment implies separation – there are two separate entities which become fixed together, like two objects stuck together with glue. But if you really love someone, there is no separation between the two of you, and so no attachment. Rather than being attached to them, you're actually *one* with them.

Unfortunately, though, this kind of love is quite rare; most relationships contain some element of need or dependence. In fact, this is one of the major sources of conflict in relationships, when our partners aren't able to give us what we need, or when they sense that we're clinging to them and so feel weighed down by the responsibility.

It may be difficult to imagine, but all of your attachments are really nothing to do with *you*. Your ambitions, beliefs, knowledge, past achievements, success, career, roles and possessions are not you – they're only accoutrements you've added to yourself, in the same way that the clothes you put on your body are not the body itself. You can gain an inkling of this by asking yourself, 'Where are my achievements, my knowledge, my ambitions, my wealth, my success or my beliefs right at this moment?' None of them *are* a part of the present moment – they're all just abstractions, mental concepts which you have to think into existence. All you are and all you have at this present moment is your *awareness* – of your own being and of your surroundings.

Perhaps there was a time in your life when you took on certain beliefs. Perhaps you were reading about some ideas that made sense to you and suddenly it occurred to you that this meant you were a socialist, an atheist, a Christian or a Muslim. And somehow the very fact of attaching these beliefs and that label to yourself made you feel more defined as a person, somehow stronger. You might have experienced something similar with ambitions or hopes. Perhaps there was a time when you were depressed and frustrated, and in response your mind created pipe dreams for you to cling to – the hope that you were going to win the lottery, or meet the man or woman of your dreams, or save up some money and go to live abroad, or be a famous pop star or actor. Again, with these hopes to cling to, suddenly you felt stronger and your predicament seemed more bearable.

Perhaps you can recognize this with your job or profession, compared to when you were a student. Back then you probably felt a little unsure of yourself, as if you didn't have a strong sense of identity. But now you know exactly who you are: you're a teacher or lawyer, a journalist or IT manager, as well as a husband or wife and father or mother – and these roles have given you a more solid sense of identity, a stronger sense of self.

These attachments are the building blocks of the ego. They make us feel stronger and more secure. They make us feel significant, that we're 'someone' and that our life has value. And the more of them we have, the stronger the ego becomes, and the more important we feel.

BREAKING ATTACHMENTS

However, every so often, these attachments are broken. This is always painful at first, of course, but after a while you may become aware of a liberating effect.

Think about what happens when your hopes or beliefs are dashed, for example – when you don't get the promotion you were hoping for, or even when you lose your job, when you realize that you're not going to make it as a singer or actor after all, or when you realize that the religious beliefs you took for granted don't have any foundation. After a few days or weeks, your initial disappointment and disillusionment may give way to a feeling of inner strength, as if the part of yourself which you gave away to these attachments is given back to you. Or this might happen at the end of a relationship – after a few weeks, the turmoil and pain may subside and give way to a new sense of freedom and wholeness, as if you have 'come back to yourself'. After giving so much of your life and your being to the other person and depending on them for your happiness and security, you realize that you're strong enough to cope on your own after all, that in a sense you don't need your ex-partner or anyone else. Or you might have this feeling after giving up a mild addiction, like smoking, coffee or junk food. After the initial struggle, you might feel yourself become stronger and more whole – as if, again, you were giving a part of yourself away to the addiction and that part has now been given back to you.

One story which illustrates the positive effects of detachment very graphically was given to me by a man who lost all his possessions. A few years ago, he moved to Barcelona to begin a contract job, but within minutes of arriving at the airport all his luggage was stolen, including his wallet, with his money and the contact details for his job in it. At first he was in a state of panic, wondering how he was going to survive. He didn't speak Spanish and didn't know anyone in the city. At first, he approached people at the airport, telling them what had happened and asking for money, but no one believed him. He went to the police, but they were unhelpful too. For the first few nights he slept rough on the streets, or on the beach, and stole food from finished plates outside restaurants.

However, once the initial panic and fear faded away, he felt a strange sense of well-being. One night, after about two weeks of being homeless, he fell asleep on the beach with a feeling of liberation inside him and a sense of being – in his words – 'in tune' with a deeper part of himself. As a Buddhist, he recognized that this was a spiritual feeling, connected to 'letting go of my normal identity and status'. From this point, his perceptions seemed different too – his surroundings seemed more real and beautiful. Eventually he went to the British Embassy, who loaned him the money for a return flight, but he felt no hurry to go back home – in fact, he waited another week before buying a ticket.

The American author Henry Miller had a similar experience. In his early thirties, he was living in New York, newly married and working as an employment manager for a telegraph company. However, he'd always had a burning desire to be a writer and decided to give everything up and go to Europe. He went to Paris and lived in squalor there for over a year. He had no money, often slept rough and sometimes went without food for whole days. His wife was supposed to join him there and kept promising to send him money to keep him afloat until she arrived, but neither she nor the money ever came.

At first Miller was lonely and despondent, but slowly he began to feel that he was undergoing a kind of purgation, a process of – in his words – 'picking himself clean'. He came to realize that 'there was nothing to hope for ... all my life I had been looking forward to something happening, some intrinsic event that would alter my life, and now suddenly, inspired by the absolute hopelessness of everything, I felt relieved, felt as though a great burden had been lifted from my shoulders'. He decided that from now on – like shifters such as Kevin, Michael and Irene – he was no longer going to try to *make* things happen in his life, but would 'let myself drift with the tide ... make not the slightest resistance to fate'.[2] At this point, he is 'naked as a savage ... a skeleton'.[3]

In other words, Miller went through a process of detachment. The squalor and desolation he experienced broke his psychological attachments – to his wife, his possessions, his money, his future, his status and his identity as a professional, cultured person. He reduced himself to a skeleton to find a wholeness and serenity at the core of his being. As he writes, 'I have no money, no resources. No hopes. I am the happiest man alive.'[4] (In view of the connection between suffering and creativity, it's perhaps not surprising that this period of detachment was also when Miller found himself as a writer and began to write *Tropic of Cancer*.)

Another acquaintance told me how, after many years of unhappiness, she finally began to feel a sense of well-being in her late forties, when she went into her menopause. Part of the reason for this was, she believes, because she lost her attachment to her appearance. As a younger woman, she had always been beautiful and had a lot of attention from men. As a result, her sense of identity had been bound up with her appearance; she'd always made an effort to look as good as possible, wearing a lot of make-up and spending a lot of time shopping for clothes. Being thought of as beautiful made her feel special.

At first, when she realized that her beauty was fading and that men were no longer as attracted to her, she felt a sense of loss. But soon this switched to a sense of liberation, as she began to realize that she didn't actually *need* the attention. She began to let go of her attachment to her appearance and realized that, by placing so much emphasis on it, she'd lost touch with her true identity. She began to feel more authentic and much happier, finding a deeper source of well-being inside herself.

In fact, it's quite common for a process of detachment to occur as people approach old age. In addition to losing our attachment to our appearance, we often lose our attachment to hopes and ambitions. We realize that we don't have much time left and stop imagining alternative futures for ourselves. We stop striving to become something else and begin to accept ourselves and our lives as they are. When we retire, we also give up our attachment to our career, along with the status and identity that gives us. And now that our children have left home, we lose our role as parents too.

Some people don't accept the loss of these things: they become bitter in their old age, wishing they were still young and attractive, that they still had their job to make them feel valued and important, or that their life had turned out differently. But as a result of this process of detachment, many older people become more contented. Research on the happiness of different age groups in the UK has found – surprisingly, it might seem at first – that the happiest age group is the over-sixties. Happiness levels are quite high in the twenties, then dip through the thirties and reach their lowest point in the mid-forties. But after 50, they start to rise, and continue rising through the sixties, when they become even higher than young people's.[5]

Similarly, a recent worldwide survey found that, so long as they are in fairly good health, 70-year-olds throughout the world are on average as happy and mentally healthy as 20-year-olds. One of the researchers, Andrew Oswald, hinted at the importance of detachment in this by suggesting that one of the reasons for old people's contentment was that 'individuals learn to adapt to their strengths and weaknesses, and in mid-life quell their infeasible aspirations'.[6]

TURMOIL AND DETACHMENT

These examples are a glimpse of the positive effects of letting go of psychological attachments. And in cases when *all* – or at least most of – our psychological attachments are suddenly and dramatically broken, these effects are intensified, and cause the psychological transformation we've been examining throughout this book.

At first, of course, the negative effects are intensified too. When all your attachments dissolve, the whole structure of the ego collapses and you feel desperate and devastated. You've lost the things you depended on for your well-being and security, everything that told you that you were important and significant, everything that defined you as a human being. You realize that your ambitions and hopes were illusions, that your beliefs were false, that your achievements are meaningless. Your career, your role in society, your status and wealth have been taken away, destroying your self-image as a successful person. The people whose love or friendship you need have rejected you. As a result, you're broken, empty, devastated. Your whole identity has been destroyed.

All of the shifters experienced major loss of this kind, or at least were threatened with major loss through encountering death. Cheryl recognized that the main reason for her depression was not being able to work, which took away her status and self-worth. Jamie lost her husband, her house and savings, and then her daughter (who went to live with her ex-husband). Stephanie lost her baby when she was 25 and then, after a long series of other misfortunes, lost a partner she thought was her soulmate. Glyn also suffered the loss of bereavement and then the loss of her business and her savings. In addition, she went through two years of intense stress and anxiety after her daughter's death.

Gill Hicks had to face the loss of her limbs and the other types of loss this entailed – the loss of her mobility and independence and activities she had enjoyed. Michael Hutchison suffered the most severe loss of anyone in this book – first of all, the loss of practically all his possessions (including his manuscripts) when his house burnt down and then the loss of the use of all his limbs, leading to the loss of almost every activity he enjoyed, including writing, reading, talking and making love. (At the same time, like Glyn, Michael suffered from intense depression and frustration after his accident, particularly from not being able to do anything except stare at the ceiling.)

Kevin lost almost everything because of his alcoholism – his family, his house, his money and his job. Bill Wilson, the founder of Alcoholics Anonymous, was in a similar state when every external kind of support – relationships, status, hopes and illusions – had dissolved away, destroyed by his addiction, so that he was completely desolate. In the words of the psychologist Stan Grof – speaking generally of addicts who reach 'rock bottom' – 'the person is left naked, with nothing but the core of his or her being'.[7]

But at this point of devastation and desolation, you are, paradoxically, close to a state of liberation. You're now in a state of *de*tachment. The building blocks of the ego have been torn away and the structure of the normal psyche has dissolved. And this state of emptiness allows a new self to be born.

Sometimes this is only temporary. In some cases, the old self is just in abeyance, dormant rather than actually dead. Its structure has dissolved, but its mould still exists, so that it can re-emerge and re-form. This is what happens in temporary awakening experiences, such as those we looked at in Chapter 1.

But in many other cases – those where suffering has been very intense over a longer period – the mould of the old self does dissolve completely. The new higher self crystallizes, rising like a phoenix from the ashes of the old. What Karlfried Graf von Dürckheim called the 'ego-shell' is broken down and 'true being' is able to flow through. Sometimes this new self forms slowly, emerging over months and years as the mould of the normal psyche gradually fades away. (We looked at examples of this 'post-traumatic growth' in Chapter 1, including Cheryl's, Iris's and Carrie's stories.) But as we've seen, in most cases the shift is instantaneous. The ego-shell breaks open suddenly, giving birth to a new self straight away.

The shift can also be interpreted in terms of energy. As I mentioned at the beginning of the last chapter, our normal ego – including all of the psychological attachments that bolster it – uses up a massive amount of energy, both in its activity (mainly through its constant thought-chatter) and as a structure. And so, when psychological attachments dissolve and the normal ego itself fades away, there is a massive intensification of our life-energy. All the energy that is normally dissipated is collected inside us; the 'powers of the soul' are given back to us. As a result, we have a sudden feeling of inner wholeness and strength, a new clarity and openness. And if the normal ego dissolves permanently, this state of intensified energy also becomes permanent. We shift into a permanent ISLE state, a state of intensified and stilled life-energy, and therefore a permanent state of spiritual experience.

In a sense this self isn't wholly new – it was always there, as our deepest, truest nature, beneath the maze of our psychological attachments and the turbulence of our thoughts and emotions. But now that deeper self becomes our normal self.

ACCEPTANCE

If the breaking of psychological attachments is normally a painful process, when – and how – does it switch to a state of liberation and transformation?

The important concept here is *acceptance*. Detachment becomes a positive, transformational state when it is *accepted*. If you resist it, fight it and try to push it away, then you'll keep feeling the pain of your broken psychological attachments. But eventually you might reach a point where you're too tired to carry on fighting, or where you realize that resistance is futile anyway, or where you just accept your predicament as fate or the will of God – and that's the point where transformation takes place.

If this transformation is seen as a 'spiritual alchemy', then acceptance is the chemical agent that brings it about. As Eckhart Tolle puts it:

> *Whenever any disaster strikes, or something goes*
> *seriously 'wrong' – illness, disability, loss of home*
> *or fortune or of a socially defined identity, break-up*
> *of a close relationship, death or suffering of a loved*
> *one, or your own impending death – know that there*
> *is another side to it, that you are just one step away*
> *from something incredible: a complete alchemical*
> *transformation of the base metal of pain and suffering*
> *into gold. That one step is called surrender.*[8]

For many of the shifters, there was a single identifiable point where they surrendered to their predicament in this way. Jamie's transformation occurred after she had decided that her situation was hopeless and that she should just accept it and expect nothing better. In a very similar way, Stephanie's transformation occurred when she 'gave up' and decided there was no point striving for anything else in her life. Berta's happened after she had begun to accept her illness and integrate it into her life, while Michael's took place when, after months of frustration, he heard a voice inside his head say, 'Let go.' For Kevin, it was when he realized that his drinking problem was too big for him to deal with and 'handed it over' to a higher power.

DEATH AND DETACHMENT

Detachment is also the major reason why encounters with death can lead to transformation. Death breaks psychological attachments in a more powerful and dramatic way than any other event – which is precisely why it has such a powerful awakening effect.

At the same time, this is why confronting death can be such a terrifying experience – it threatens to take *everything* away from us. If you know you only have a certain amount of time left to live, the future closes down, dissolving all your hopes and ambitions. You're stripped of every externality, every accoutrement, everything that defined your identity or gave you security and well-being. You're literally reduced to nothing.

Many people who face death don't go beyond this, and die in a state of bitterness and disappointment. But again, once this state is *accepted*, transformation occurs.

Imminent death is more likely to generate acceptance than any other type of trauma or turmoil, simply because if you know that you're going to die soon, you're *forced* to accept it. With any other kind of loss, there's usually some opportunity to persuade yourself that things are going to get better. There are always hopes or beliefs to hold on to. But with death this isn't possible: everything your ego clings to will be stripped away, whether you like it or not.

Usually the acceptance of imminent death develops gradually. Elisabeth Kübler-Ross, the pioneering death researcher whose work led to the hospice movement, suggested that people who know they are going to die go through five stages of grief: anger, denial, bargaining, depression and finally acceptance.[9] Most of the shifters who transformed through encountering death – for example, Iris, Dennis Potter, Val, Hugh Martin, Treya Killam Wilber and William Murtha – seem to have been through a similar process, with long periods of bitterness and depression gradually giving way to acceptance – and, as a consequence, a state of liberation.

In other cases, however, the acceptance of death was a sudden event. For Winifred Holtby, it occurred at the point where she heard a voice inside her head say, 'Having nothing, yet possessing all things.' At that moment, all of the sadness and bitterness she had felt at her imminent death disappeared, and never came back. For Irene, it happened straightaway, as soon as she was diagnosed with cancer, and so she underwent transformation straightaway too.

Karlfried Graf von Dürckheim noted that the cases of transformation he came across during the Second World War occurred when the soldiers, concentration camp inmates and refugees accepted their predicament, including the fact that they were probably going to die. As he described it:

Many of us have experienced the nearness of death – in air raids, illness, or at other times of mortal danger – and have found that if, at the very moment when terror engulfs us and our inner resistance collapses, we can somehow submit and accept ... we are suddenly calm, our fears are instantly forgotten, and we have the certainty that there is something in us that death and destruction cannot touch... We are suddenly, inexplicably conscious of a new and invincible strength. We do not know its source or its purpose – we only know that we are standing in it, that it encloses us utterly. This is a sign that Being has touched us, and been able to penetrate our innermost being, because the shell we had fashioned for ourselves – and that cuts us off from it – has been atomized.[10]

WHY IS SUFFERING TRANSFORMATIONAL FOR SOME, BUT NOT FOR OTHERS?

This discussion helps us to understand one of the most puzzling aspects of SITEs: why do they happen to some people but not others? Why do some people just suffer, whereas for others suffering leads to liberation? Is there, for example, a particular kind of person who is more likely to have a SITE?

One important factor is the degree to which a person directly *faces* their predicament. Understandably, many people who go through turmoil and trauma – especially people who are seriously ill and/or going to die – try to avoid contemplating their situation. This is their way of trying to cope with it – they try to block it out of their mind, to distract themselves from it. Or they might be in denial about their illness, deluding themselves that it isn't as serious as it seems.

This is natural, of course, but it seems that this avoidance reduces the potential for transformation. The psychologists Les Lancaster and Jason Palframan investigated a number of people's responses to traumatic events such as illness, alcoholism and domestic abuse. They found that people who tended to avoid thinking or talking about their problem were less likely to experience post-traumatic growth. People who did face up to their situation and accept it, however, did develop in a positive way. They described themselves as being more serene and at ease with themselves, and feeling as though there was more meaning and purpose in their life.[11]

This suggests that two personal qualities which increase the likelihood of transformation are *courage* and *realism*. People who are more courageous are more likely to face up to their predicament, with all the anxiety and horror that may entail (at least initially). At the same time, people who are more realistic are less likely to delude themselves with false hopes. The kind of people who – for example – have a habit of romanticizing their past, daydreaming about alternative life situations or idyllic futures are more likely to use escapism as a way of trying to cope with trauma and turmoil.

Having the courage and realism to face up to our predicament is the first stage of acceptance – which, as we've seen, is the most important factor of all. Not everyone moves from facing up to acceptance, though. Whether a person is able to do so may depend, again, on their personality. People who have a strong need to be 'in control' – people who like to be decisive and powerful and feel that they are consciously directing the course of their life – are less likely to accept loss or illness and so less likely to experience transformation.

Kevin Hinchcliffe is very aware of this in his work counselling cancer patients. He regularly comes across patients who aren't prepared to let go and who therefore become bitter and depressed. As he told me:

> There's a type of person we call 'the controllers'. You can see them straightaway. It's reflected in their jobs – they're often head teachers, solicitors, heads of organizations in powerful positions. They are very used to control; they need it for their own security. Cancer comes along and because they have no control over it, they fall apart. It asks them to look at life differently, but some of them will not relinquish control. They fight it and it's the resistance that causes the anguish.
>
> You can see this reflected in their well-being and ultimately in their illness. In my experience, people who are willing to let go are more likely to recover.

In other words, people who are more easy-going and unassuming and less domineering are more likely to experience transformation, because they're more likely to relinquish control and to develop an attitude of acceptance.

These concepts of facing up and acceptance are closely linked to Kübler-Ross' five stages of dealing with imminent death. Some people don't move beyond the first two stages of anger and denial, but if they do, they progress to the stages of bargaining and then depression. At the latter stage, their depression stems from facing up to their predicament and becoming aware of the enormity and finality of death. Many people don't move beyond this point either, but if they do, they progress to the final stage of acceptance.

Another aspect of personality which seems to affect people's potential to have a SITE is whether they are left- or right-brain oriented. Shifters tend to be right-brain oriented. They're more likely to be creative and sensitive people, the kind of people who make decisions intuitively rather than logically and who have 'hunches' or ideas which seem to come out of nowhere.

Some evidence for this was provided by William Miller and Janet C'de Baca, who interviewed over 50 people who believed they had undergone a sudden spiritual transformation. Miller and C'de Baca also become very aware of SITEs: more than half of the transformations they examined happened in response to intense unhappiness or in the midst of tragedy – for example, people who were suffering from the post-traumatic effects of childhood abuse, who were seriously ill, deeply depressed or addicted to alcohol or drugs. (The other cases were apparently the result of a long period of spiritual practice or had no apparent cause at all.) But most significantly, Miller and C'de Baca asked the 'quantum changers' to complete a personality test, which found that around two-thirds of them had a predominantly 'intuitive' personality.[12]

An early American psychologist named Professor George Coe reached a similar conclusion about religious conversion. After interviewing 77 people who had undergone conversion, he found it was more likely to happen to people who had, in his words, an 'active subliminal self' – that is, people who had more access to their subconscious mind. Converts were usually highly emotional people who could be hypnotized easily and often had strange impulses, strong intuitive feelings and the ability to do automatic writing or speech.[13] In other words, they were people whose conscious mind had more labile boundaries and so was open to information and impulses from other parts of the psyche. I've suggested that there are important differences between SITEs and religious conversion, but I think that this personality type is probably one of the similarities.

Perhaps, however, both of these characteristics – a less controlling personality and a more right-brain orientation – are expressions of the same underlying factor: a less powerful ego. After all, the desire for control and power is closely associated with a strong ego structure. A strong ego structure means a strong sense of separation and incompleteness, which creates a strong need for reinforcement through status and power. Similarly, having a more 'labile' conscious mind – and therefore being more open to emotion, intuition and creativity – is equivalent to having a weaker ego structure.

The ego is also linked to the left side of the brain. That's where it seems to live, and typical left-brain characteristics such as logic, practicality, literalness and scepticism towards the new can be seen as aspects of the ego's functioning. So a more right-brain-oriented person is likely to have a weaker ego.

So perhaps what we should say is that SITEs are more likely to happen to people whose egos are weaker. And this is completely logical, of course: the weaker the ego, the more easily it will be dislodged by turmoil and trauma. A person with a strong ego is less likely to 'cave in' to the pressure of suffering – they'll keep trying to control their predicament and feel depressed and frustrated because they can't. At the same time, because of their strong ego boundaries, they'll be less open to energies and impulses from outside their conscious mind. On the other hand, a weaker ego is more likely to dissolve, in the same way that a flimsy building is more likely to collapse in a hurricane than a sturdy, reinforced structure.

WOMEN AND SITES

This relates to another significant point about SITEs: women seem to be more likely to have them than men. Of the 33 people I interviewed for this book, only ten were men. In particular, women seem to be much more likely to have a transformational experience triggered by illness, stress, upheaval, bereavement and disability. In Chapters 2 to 4, I describe ten of these experiences and only feature one man, Michael. (I actually interviewed two other women who had SITEs after intense stress and depression, but didn't include them in the book.)

This makes sense in terms of the explanation I've just put forward. Generally speaking, women have a weaker ego structure than men. This is why women tend to be more empathic than men, and why men tend to have a more 'systematizing brain'. Research has shown, for example, than women are better at reading emotions from people's expressions than men and have a more supportive and empathic conversational style.[14]

In *The Fall* I suggest two reasons why, in our psychological development as a species, women's egos never became as strong as men's. First, women's strong bond with their children may have stopped their egos becoming too strong and separate, because they had to keep a strong psychological connection to their children. Secondly, women's more active biology may have worked against a strong ego. Male biology is fairly quiescent; apart from hunger and sex and the occasional illness, men don't need to pay much attention to their body and so it's easy to become 'split off' from it and disappear into the mental realm of the ego. But women's more powerful biological processes – including the menstrual cycle, pregnancy and lactation – mean that they are more rooted in their body.

For these reasons, in *The Fall* I suggest that women are closer to an 'unfallen' state than men. Similarly, Eckhart Tolle suggests that because of this, women are naturally 'closer to enlightenment' than men. As he told me when I interviewed him for this book, 'The egoic shell in women is not quite as rigid as in men. The ego is a little bit less entrenched; there is a little less mind-identification. Women are more in touch with their body, with their feelings.'

ANOMALIES

I don't want to draw up any hard and fast rules about who can have SITEs and who can't, though. It's important to remember that although a weaker ego structure might make a SITE more likely, it can still happen to *anyone*. When turmoil and trauma are especially intense, a SITE can dissolve even the strongest ego, just as a powerful hurricane can destroy the sturdiest building in a town. After all, several of the shifters we've heard from were fairly materialistic and ambitious people and do seem to have had a 'controlling' nature to some degree. For example, Carrie was a successful

TV writer who liked to spend her money on her house, while Irene was a high-achieving IT manager and Tony was a successful businessman.

At the same time, there are some ways in which SITEs don't seem to follow any regular pattern. For example, you might assume that since they're a form of spiritual transformation, they would be more likely to happen to people who were already 'spiritual' to some degree, people who were already meditating, doing yoga or following other spiritual paths. But this doesn't seem to be the case. The only person I interviewed who had a clear interest in spirituality before his transformation is Michael, who was the author of books on science and spirituality. None of the other shifters had any real knowledge of spirituality and some of them had even tended to be a little disparaging towards it. (Janice told me, 'I used to think it was all self-indulgent rubbish for people who couldn't think rationally.')

You might also think that physical pain would make SITEs less likely to occur. How could someone possibly experience a state of liberation when their body was damaged by illness or injury and as a result they were in acute pain or discomfort? Surely, you might think, that could only happen at an early stage of an illness like cancer, before the pain and other physical problems become serious, or later, during remission. But this isn't the case either. Several of the shifters were in real pain when they had their SITE. For example, Cheryl was seriously ill with ME and Gill Hicks was struggling with the pain of losing her limbs. The best example of this is Michael Hutchison, who still suffers from acute neuralgic pain now, due to the damage to his vertebrae. He has learned to 'drop into' a state of pure consciousness to manage his pain and, as I noted earlier, is so successful at this that he has refused his doctors' offer of a permanent morphine drip in his spine.

It seems that pain isn't a barrier to transformation. In fact, there are *no* barriers to the experience. As long as you have an ego, and as long as that ego is supported by psychological attachments, it's possible that at some point trauma and turmoil will come your way and tear those attachments away, reducing you to nothing and, at the same time, shifting you into a higher state of being.

12

BREAKING
FREE

After reading these accounts of people who've undergone transformation after intense turmoil and trauma or through close encounters with death, you might be thinking, 'This is all very interesting, but what does it mean *for me?*' What relevance does it have for those of us who are living relatively secure and contented lives? After all, no one would seriously recommend making a *conscious* effort to bring turmoil and trauma into their life or stage an encounter with death.

Nevertheless, there are some very important lessons we can learn from the shifters' experiences and some ways in which we can follow their lead without actually inflicting suffering on ourselves. In this final chapter, I'm going to suggest three of these: conscious detachment, spiritual practice and developing an awareness of death.

CONSCIOUS DETACHMENT

If we know that the awakening effect of turmoil or an encounter with death is due to the dissolving of psychological attachments, then perhaps we can live our lives in such a way that we're relatively free of attachments. Perhaps we can simply make a conscious effort to detach ourselves.

In fact, this is something that spiritual seekers throughout history have attempted to do. This is the root of the traditional spiritual practice of renunciation, for example. Renunciation means relinquishing family life and sex (by being celibate), worldly pleasures and personal ambitions. Spiritual seekers also expected to practise 'voluntary poverty' – that is, to have a bare minimum of possessions, not to own any property and to live without any unnecessary comforts. This is the basis of the monastic way of life: monks and nuns give up everything in their quest for spiritual development, or enlightenment.

From a modern (or post-modern) perspective, renunciation seems unhealthy. It implies a duality between 'the spirit' and 'the world', as if there's something innately *un*spiritual about the world of relationships, sex, family and work, and that spiritual development is only possible through rejecting all of them. But surely – and this is my personal view – this distinction is false. A true spirituality should be part of the everyday world and encompass every aspect of our life, especially our relationships.

Nevertheless, the goal of renunciation is to create a state of detachment. By renouncing 'the world', monks and mystics are trying to avoid developing any psychological attachments. They're consciously trying to create a state of 'having nothing, possessing everything', the state of nakedness that Henry Miller found himself in after arriving in Paris or the state of desolation that Kevin found himself in after his life fell apart due to his alcoholism. By 'emptying their souls' in this way, they're trying to ensure that they don't build up a superficial ego self which would obscure their true spiritual self. Or, in terms of energy, they're trying to intensify the 'powers of the soul' by making sure that they aren't dissipated by psychological attachments.

In the Christian mystical tradition, the connection between detachment and spiritual awakening is especially strong. Detachment was a part of the process of 'purgation' (also including asceticism), which led to a state of 'illumination', the point at which the mystic first awakened to the divine reality. Some mystics ended their development there, but for others illumination was followed by the 'Dark Night of the Soul', the terrible state in which the mystic felt abandoned by the divine. But the Dark Night of the Soul was a process of *further* detachment. After breaking their attachment to the world of possessions and ambitions, now the mystics had to break the final attachment: to their own ego. If they did this, they reached the final mystical state of deification, or union, and became one with the divine.

Needless to say, I don't believe it's necessary for us to go to these extremes. It's possible to be free of psychological attachments to a large degree without rejecting 'the world' and shutting ourselves up in monasteries or going to live in the desert. We can do this simply by identifying our attachments and consciously trying to reduce our dependency on them. For example, you might be aware that you're attached to possessions or money. You might enjoy the feeling of buying 'nice' things, of owning jewellery and expensive ornaments and of impressing other people with your fashionable clothes and beautiful house. Similarly, you might be able to identify a strong attachment to your appearance, so that you feel the need to look good in order to feel good about yourself. Or, closely linked to this, you might be aware that you're attached to your youth. The idea of getting old may depress you, so that you try hard to make yourself look younger. Or perhaps you might feel attached to the home environment you've grown up in and the people you've known all your life, so that you feel slightly threatened by the wider world.

Giving up any attachment feels uncomfortable at first and brings a sense of lack or insecurity. This is natural – after all, the attachment has been helping to prop up the ego, so that we feel fragile without it, like a child without stabilizers on their bike for the first time. But in the same way that a child learns to balance on the bike, we quickly grow stronger and find that we didn't really need the attachment after all. Our true self seems to grow into the space left by it, giving us a greater sense of wholeness and well-being. If you make a conscious effort to 'downshift' by no longer buying unnecessary things, or take the decision to no longer invest so much time and attention in your appearance, you'll probably be surprised at how strong and liberated this makes you feel.

To a large extent, this is a question of realizing that we shouldn't rely on external things for our well-being. Attention, possessions, success and status can give us a kind of happiness, but it's a very temporary and fragile one. It usually only comes in short bursts, which we quickly grow used to, so that we need bigger and bigger 'fixes'. But by 'slaking off' our attachments, we exchange this temporary happiness for access to the deeper and richer – and much more stable – well-being of our own true selves.

SPIRITUAL PRACTICE

However, it's also important to go deeper and address the root cause of our need for psychological attachments: our fragile and separate ego, which needs to be reinforced by attachments. We can reduce our need for attachments by working on the ego directly and attempting to heal its separateness and sense of lack. Perhaps the most effective way of doing this is through meditation. In fact, this is the basic aim of meditation: to weaken the ego as a structure so that its boundaries become softer and so that our normal sense of separation and isolation is replaced by a sense of connection and wholeness.

Mindfulness exercises and meditative physical exercises such as yoga or *t'ai chi* can achieve a similar healing effect. Acts of service – such as bringing up children, doing charity or community work, counselling or teaching – can soften the boundaries of the ego too, enabling us to transcend self-centredness and develop a strong sense of empathy and connection with others. Or for a formal and structured approach, we could follow a recognized spiritual path, such as the Buddhist, Tantric or Taoist ways. Essentially, every spiritual path is a movement beyond ego-separateness towards connection and union.

Any path or practice which helps you to cultivate an inner well-being and wholeness will reduce your need for psychological attachments. You won't need them any more in the same way that a completed building doesn't need scaffolding or support.

CULTIVATING AN AWARENESS OF DEATH

Perhaps the most effective way of developing a state of detachment, however, is by cultivating an awareness of death. We've seen that encountering death is one of the most powerful ways of dissolving psychological attachments, and it's possible to harness this transformational power without actually risking dying.

We're taught that death is something we should shy away from and try to forget about. And it's certainly true that becoming aware of death can create anxiety and depression. But there's a difference between being aware of death as a concept and being confronted with the *reality* of it and forced to deal with it as an imminent prospect.

This relates to the point I made in the last chapter about the importance of *facing* rather than avoiding distress and turmoil. In psychology, there's a theory called Terror Management, which suggests that a large part of all human behaviour is generated by the unconscious fear of death. This fear generates a fundamental anxiety and unease which we try to offset with behaviour such as seeking status or strongly defending the values of our culture. We feel threatened by death and so seek security and significance to defend ourselves against it. Studies have shown, for example, that when people are made more aware of their own mortality, they tend to become more nationalistic and tribal and more materialistic.[1]

However, this is just what happens when we're *passively* aware of death, without confronting it as a reality. When we face up to it actively and directly, there's a good chance that we'll transcend this anxiety and insecurity and experience its full transformational potential. Paradoxically, as we saw in the last chapter, facing up to our own mortality fully may *release* us from the fear of death.

One way in which we can do this without actually endangering our life is through undergoing a kind of *simulated* death. For example, the transpersonal psychologist Stan Grof, working together with his wife Christina, has found that in non-ordinary states of consciousness induced by LSD or breathing exercises, it's possible for individuals to relive the experience of being born. In Grof's view, the process of birth has such strong parallels with the process of dying that to relive your own birth also means to experience your own death. As a result, he speaks of the 'death-rebirth' experience. According to him, those who undergo this experience are permanently transformed. The filters that restrict their normal awareness fall away, so that perception becomes much more intense. Nothing is familiar or taken for granted. As Grof writes:

> *We may feel that we are really seeing the world for the first time in our lives. Everything around us, even the most ordinary and familiar scenes, seems unusually exacting and stimulating. People report entirely new ways of appreciating and enjoying their loved ones, the sound of music, the beauties of nature.*[2]

Their time orientation also changes – the future and past become much less important than the present. But most significantly, Grof also describes them as becoming free of psychological attachments, aware of the 'futility of exaggerated ambitions, attachment to money, status, fame and power'.[3] In other words, the effects are exactly the same as actually encountering death.

But even more simply, we can achieve a similar effect by *imagining* our own death – or, more strictly, imagining that we only have a certain amount of time left to live. The poet and author Stephen Levine did this as an experiment. After spending 25 years working with the dying as a counsellor and therapist, he was well aware of the positive effects of encountering death and always thought it a terrible shame that these only occurred at the *end* of a person's life. So he and his wife decided to tell themselves that they were going to die exactly a year from that moment and live as if that really were the case.

During his 'final' year, Levine reviewed his life and felt ashamed of some of the things he'd done, but at the same time felt compassion towards his younger self. He forgave the people who'd wronged him, repaired his relationships with people he'd fallen out with and renewed old friendships. He found that he felt increased gratitude for his life and had a heightened sense of presence and of beauty. At the end of the year, he reflected that:

> *My life has changed in subtle and unexpected ways. My sense of time has changed – there seems to be more of the present. A new found energy has been liberated... My relationships with friends have deepened, and in some cases, blossomed again. Afflictive emotions, particularly to do with the past, have become considerably less cumbersome. And love is more available and sustainable. It feels as though I have made peace with my life.*[4]

In addition to facing up to our *own* mortality, it's important to face death fully when it happens to people around us. When relatives and friends die, we shouldn't be tempted to try to distract ourselves from our grief but allow ourselves to feel the loss and emptiness of bereavement, however painful it might be. It's important to contemplate the full of meaning of the person's death and to be aware that the same thing is going to happen to us at some point.

This is the purpose of the 'cemetery meditations' recommended in Buddhism. In the *Satipatthana Sutta*, the Buddha tells his monks that if they see a dead body, whether it is one that is newly dead, one being eaten by animals or one that's nothing more than a skeleton or a pile of bones, they should tell themselves: 'Verily, also my own body is of the same nature; such it will become and will not escape it.' In this way, the monk becomes aware of the impermanence of life and, in the Buddha's words, 'lives detached, and clings to nothing in the world'.[5]

It's also important to share the company of relatives and friends who are dying. Again, we might be tempted to shy away from the reality of their predicament and be afraid of awkwardness and embarrassment. But as well as being a great comfort to them, sharing their company will intensify our own awareness of death as we watch them preparing to take a journey which we'll also be making at some point.

This is why working with the dying – as a counsellor, nurse or hospice volunteer – can be a profound experience. In Chapter 7, we saw how working as a hospice volunteer changed Paul McDermott's life, giving him a new spiritual awareness and positive attitude towards death. It's quite common for hospice workers to be affected in this way. Being so close to death on a daily basis is a powerful spur for their personal development. A friend of mine who was a hospice nurse described how 'as they get nearer to death, people don't pretend any more. They drop all their masks and become who they really are. They become honest and vulnerable. And once you experience that in others, you can't play roles yourself any more. You have to be completely authentic in every aspect of your life.' For her, being a hospice nurse – or a 'midwife for the dying' as she calls it – was a great privilege. 'After you've helped someone to die, it teaches you a lot,' she says. 'On one level, you're aware of how precious life is – too precious to waste doing things you don't want to do. But there's a meaning to it as well. The sense of connection makes you feel that there's something more, a deeper dimension to life.'

All of these methods have the same basic principle: they're all just different ways of *reminding ourselves* of our own mortality. It's actually quite difficult for us to remember death, partly because of our death-denying culture, but also because of the limitations of our mind. The mind is designed to focus on present and immediate realities rather than bigger and more abstract ones such as death. It has a microscopic focus, whereas death is a macrocosmic reality. (This is also why it's so difficult for us to treat environmental problems with the full seriousness they deserve.)

As a consequence, it's important for us to make a *conscious* effort to remind ourselves of death. If you're not able to try the methods I've suggested above, at least spend a few minutes of every day thinking about your own death, contemplating the fact that you're only on this planet for a certain amount of time, that death could strike you down at any moment and that when it does, all of your possessions, achievements, status and knowledge will dissolve into nothing. As Sogyal Rinpoche puts it in *The Tibetan Book of Living and Dying*, 'It is important to reflect calmly, again and again, that *death is real, and comes without warning.*'[6]

This may seem morbid to some people, but it's really only a question of facing up to reality. Ultimately, we're all in the same position as a cancer patient who's been told they only have a certain amount of time left to live – it's just that we don't know *how much* time we have left and it's likely that most of us will have more time than the cancer patient. Even if there is life after death – and I personally believe that there is, in some form – it doesn't change the fact that when *this* life ends we'll be separated from everything and everyone we know. Death is always present, and its transformational power is always accessible to us, as long as we're courageous enough to face it. And the more real it becomes to us, the weaker and fewer our psychological attachments will be.

So, by cultivating this awareness of death at the same time as practising conscious detachment and meditation (or another form of spiritual practice), it's possible that we'll weaken our superficial ego self to such an extent that we'll remain permanently connected to the higher, truer self beneath it. Deprived of its building blocks, the ego will then be unable to obscure and suppress our higher self.

THE END OF SUFFERING

All of the experiences we've looked at illustrate the amazing, infinite reserves of the human spirit. No matter how deep into suffering and misery we plunge, no matter how much hardship the world can send our way, even if we lose our health, our friends or partners, our possessions and careers, the use of our limbs – we aren't just able to *cope* with these terrible events, we're able to *transcend* them. The most devastating experiences and events may be able to damage us temporarily, but they don't have to destroy us. On the contrary, in times of suffering, an alchemical agent is released inside us that transmutes trauma and hardship into joy and serenity, and tragedy into spiritual awakening.

Most of us live in fear – of death, of being left by our partner, of becoming ill, of losing our job, our success and possessions, of the future, and so on. But the stories we've looked at teach us that all of this fear is misplaced. As long as we're prepared to face up to pain and suffering, there is nothing for us to be afraid of. Even the most traumatic experiences – like cancer, bereavement or becoming severely disabled – have an underlying positivity. Beneath their terrible, painful surface there is a massive reservoir of spiritual potential.

Several of the shifters I spoke to told me that they felt lucky to have gone through such trauma and turmoil, because if they hadn't, they wouldn't have experienced the transformation that followed. I would never be so patronizing as to say that anyone who goes through intense suffering is 'lucky'. I would never suggest that we should welcome suffering, or seek it out. But there will always be some degree of suffering in our lives, and when it comes, we should try not to see it in wholly negative terms. We should always be aware that, buried inside it, there is an opportunity for growth and transformation.

The experiences we've looked at also illustrate how close spiritual awakening is to us. It exists as a potential inside *everyone*. It's just that normally the potential is dormant. To manifest itself, it normally has to be triggered by turmoil and trauma. However, if we know it's there, latent in the same way that a butterfly is latent inside a caterpillar, then it should be possible to release it in other ways too, for example through the kinds of psychological or spiritual practices I've just outlined.

There is nothing esoteric or otherworldly about this state. On the contrary, for those who experience it, it's completely natural and comfortable, almost a state which they *ought* to have existed in all along. In comparison, our normal psyche seems a kind of aberration, a trance-like state of disconnection and discord which should never have become normal. The shifters have woken up from this trance into a more real, meaningful and harmonious world.

And the knowledge that enlightenment is latent in *all* of us could change our perspective of the human race. The Utopian visions of New Age philosophers no longer seem so unrealistic. Since so many 'ordinary' people have already undergone this shift, it's possible to envision a world in which *everyone* has undergone it, in which enlightenment is our *normal* state. This would be a completely different world – a world in which people no longer exploit and oppress each other in their search for wealth, status and power; a world in which people are aware of the beauty and aliveness of the world around them and so respect nature rather than just seeing it as a supply of resources; a world in which people exist in a state of well-being rather than one of discord, and so no longer spend their lives trying to escape from their own selves or in a fruitless search for fulfilment; a world in which people live in harmony with themselves and with each other.

This is just a dream, of course – but it's closer to reality than I ever would have thought before writing this book.

NOTES

Introduction

1. I have used material from 31 different interviews in this book: 8 from people who had temporary awakening experiences after turmoil and 23 from people who shifted into a permanent state of wakefulness. There were two other interviews with 'shifters' which I chose not to quote from in the end, as they were very similar to experiences I'd already used.

Chapter 1

1. It's true that many of what Hardy classes as 'religious experiences' aren't strictly 'awakening experiences' in the sense that I'm using the term. For example, he includes religious visions and supernatural experiences, such as a woman's vision of her dead husband. But there are still a large number of fully fledged awakening experiences in his collection. For example, one person described the following experience to him:

    I was going through a period of doubt and disillusion with life and torn by conflict... Quite suddenly I felt lifted beyond all the turmoil and conflict. There was no visual image and I knew I was sitting on a bench

*in the park, but I felt as if I was lifted above the world
and looking down on it. The disillusion and cynicism
were gone, and I felt compassion suffusing my whole
being, compassion for all people on earth. I was
possessed by a peace that I have never felt before or
since [in Hardy, 1979, p.76].*

Raynor C. Johnson's study of spiritual experiences,
Watcher on the Hills, also includes many such examples.
For example, here a person describes how in a state of
desperation he prayed to God for help and immediately
had a powerful mystical experience:

*At a flash, the scene changed. All became alive, the
trees, the houses, the very stones became animated
with life, and all became vibrant with the life within
them. All breathed effulgent light, vivid sparkling
light, radiating out and in every direction; and not
only that but everything seemed to be connected
with everything else. Although all separate forms,
and all vibrating with their own intensity of life, yet
they all seemed to be connected by their vibrations
into one whole thing, as the different coloured parts
of a picture are yet of the same picture [in Johnson
(1959), pp.63–5].*

Chapter 2

1. Paulson and Krippner (2007), p.13. Other research
   suggests that trauma can affect our physical health too,
   making us more prone to serious life-threatening illnesses
   such as cardiovascular disease, diabetes, gastrointestinal
   disorders and cancer. This may be because trauma
   weakens the immune system (Kendall-Tackett, 2009).

2. Dorahy and Lewis, 1998
3. In van der Kolk and van der Hart, 1989, p.1
4. Paton *et al.*, 2009
5. Han, 2006
6. Tedeschi and Calhoun, 2004, p.1
7. Neal *et al.*, 1999
8. Nietzsche, 1895
9. Gibran, 1923
10. Tomich and Helgeson, 2004; Stanton *et al.*, 2006. Similarly, the psychologist Jonathan Haidt writes, 'A diagnosis of cancer is often described, in retrospect, as a wake up call, a reality check, or a turning point... The reality people often wake up to is that life is a gift they have been taking for granted' (Haidt, 2006, p.140).
11. Kastner, 1998
12. Armstrong, 2001, p.273
13. Ibid.
14. Ibid., p.294
15. In Ehrenreich, 2010
16. McNerney, 2004

Chapter 3

1. Grof, 2000, p.137
2. Shuchter, 1986
3. Klass, 1995

Chapter 4

1. Kasser, 2002
2. Brickman *et al.*, 1978
3. Schulz and Decker, 1985. However, it should be noted that a more recent study found a less significant result. Andrew Oswald and Nattavudh Powdthavee (2008)

found that in cases of moderate disability the level of adaptation was roughly 50 per cent, while in cases of severe disability, it was 30 per cent. This still suggests a high level of adaptation, but one not as significant as Schulz and Decker's study.
4. Hicks, 2007, p.23
5. Ibid., p.26
6. Ibid., p.209
7. Ibid., p.110
8. Ibid., p.209

Chapter 5

1. Hinchcliffe, 2008
2. *Alcoholics Anonymous* (The Big Book), pp.6–7
3. Ibid., p.7
4. Ibid., p.8
5. In Walsh and Vaughan, 1993, p.146

Chapter 6

1. In Lutyens, 1983, p.6
2. In Lutyens, 1975, pp.159–60
3. Ibid., p.184
4. In Lutyens, 1983, p.10
5. Ibid.
6. Krishnamurti, 1926
7. Tolle, 2001, p.2
8. In Massad, 2009
9. Ibid.
10. Ingram, 2003, p.5
11. Ibid., p.100

Chapter 7

1. 'Space: The Greening of the Astronauts', 1972
2. Ibid.
3. *In the Shadow of the Moon*, 2008
4. In 'Space: The Greening of the Astronauts', op. cit.
5. Schweikhart, 2009
6. *In the Shadow of the Moon*, op. cit.
7. In Fenwick, 1995, p.201
8. Ibid.
9. In McDermott, 2006, pp.123–4
10. Ibid., p.136
11. Ibid., p.174
12. Marriot, 2005
13. In Jeffries, 2005
14. Ibid.
15. In Wilber, 1993, p.316
16. Ibid., p.317
17. Ibid., p.356
18. In Happold, 1986, p.131
19. Ibid., p.54
20. Whitman, 1855

Chapter 8

1. Sacks, 1990, pp.241–2
2. In ibid., p.242
3. See my earlier essay, 'Lawrence the Mystic', Taylor, 2001.
4. Huxley, 1962, p.1,256
5. Ibid., p.1,249
6. Lawrence, 1993, p.651
7. Huxley, op. cit., p.1,265
8. Lawrence, op. cit., p.705
9. In Moore, 1974, p.178

10. Ibid., p.508
11. Huxley, op. cit., p.1,266
12. Ibid., p.1,265
13. Whitman, 1867
14. Lawrence, op. cit., p.676
15. Dürckheim and Prabhupada, 2009
16. Goettmann, 2010, p.7
17. Dürckheim and Prabhupada, op. cit.
18. In Watts, 1973
19. Dürckheim, 1992, p.16

Chapter 9

1. In Fenwick, 1995, p.201
2. In Hardy, 1979, p.94
3. In Philip, 2007
4. In Friend, 2003
5. In Rosen, 1975, p.291
6. Ibid.
7. Seligman, 2002
8. In Rosen, op. cit., p.292
9. Ibid.
10. Ibid.
11. Ibid.
12. Grey, 1985, p.97
13. Ibid.

Chapter 10

1. Hicks, 2007.
2. Maslow, 1970, p.163
3. James, 1902, p.189
4. Miller and C'de Baca, 2001
5. Wilber, 2000

Chapter 11

1. In Cohen, 2000, p.53
2. Miller, 1965, p.103
3. Ibid., p.104
4. Ibid., p.9
5. 'Happiness is Smile Shaped', 2009
6. Oswald and Blanchflower, 2008
7. In Walsh and Vaughan, 1993, pp.146–7
8. Tolle, 2001, p.183
9. Kübler-Ross, 2005
10. Dürckheim, 1992, p.16
11. Lancaster and Palframan, 2009
12. Miller and C'de Baca, 2001
13. In James, 1902, pp.240–41
14. Wareing, 1999; Baron-Cohen, 2003

Chapter 12

1. Solomon *et al.*, 1991; Pyszczynski *et al.*, 2004. This theory implies that since the fear of death affects us so profoundly, *becoming free* of the fear of death would also have a dramatic effect on the way we live. In fact, this is another way of interpreting the shifters' changed values and lifestyles. Their shift to a less materialistic and success-driven lifestyle, and their more empathic and holistic outlook, could be seen as the result of a reduced fear of death. In line with Terror Management Theory, becoming free of fear of death means that they don't need to reinforce their identity and security to the same extent, if at all.
2. Grof, 1993, p.77
3. Ibid.
4. Levine, 1997, p.169
5. *Sattipatthana Sutta,* 2010
6. Rinpoche, 1993, p.18

BIBLIOGRAPHY

Alcoholics Anonymous (The Big Book) (2001). New York:
Alcoholics Anonymous World Services, Inc.

Armstrong, L. (2001). *It's Not About the Bike*. London:
Yellow Jersey Press.

Barnhart, Joe Edward and Mary Ann (1981). *The New Birth:
A Naturalistic View of Religious Conversion.* Macon, GA:
Mercer University Press.

Baron-Cohen, S. (2003). *The Essential Difference: Men,
Women and the Extreme Male Brain.* London: Allen Lane.

Brickman, P., Coates, D., Janoff-Bulman, R., (1978). 'Lottery
winners and accident victims – is happiness relative?'
Journal of Personality and Social Psychology 36, 917–27.

Cohen, A. (2000). 'Ripples of the surface of being: an
interview with Eckhart Tolle.' *What is Enlightenment*? 18,
Fall/Winter.

Cryder, C. H., Kilmer, R. P., Tedeschi, R. G., Calhoun, L. G.
(2006). 'An exploratory study of posttraumatic growth
in children following a natural disaster.' *The American
Journal of Orthopsychiatry* 76(1), 65–9.

Davis, C. and McKearney, J. M. (2003). 'How do people grow
from their experience with trauma or loss?' *Journal of
Social and Clinical Psychology* 22(5), October, 477–92.

Dorahy, M. J., and Lewis, C. A. (1998). 'Trauma-induced
dissociation and the psychological effects of the

"troubles" in Northern Ireland: an overview and integration.' *Irish Journal of Psychology* 19, 332–44.

Dürckheim, K. G. von (1992). *Absolute Living: The Otherworldly in the World and the Path to Maturity.* London: Arkana.

Dürckheim, K. G. von and Prabhupada. A. C. (2009). *Changing Bodies: A Dialogue.* Retrieved 13/4/09 from http://www.harekrishna.com/col/books/KR/cb/chapter2.html.

Ehrenreich, B. (2010). 'Smile – You've Got Cancer!' *Guardian.* Retrieved from http://www.guardian.co.uk/lifeandstyle/2010/jan/02/cancer-positive-thinking-barbara-ehrenreich.

Fenwick, P. and E. (1995). *The Truth in the Light.* London: Headline.

Fontana, D. (2004). *Is There an Afterlife?* Southampton: O Books.

Fosse, Magdalena J. (2005). 'Posttraumatic growth: the transformative potential of cancer.' *Dissertation Abstracts International: Section B: The Sciences and Engineering* 66(3-B), 1,716.

Friend, T. (2003). 'Jumpers: The fatal grandeur of the Golden Gate Bridge.' *The New Yorker*, 13/10/03. Retrieved 1/2/10 from http://www.newyorker.com/archive/2003/10/13/ixzz0c3VIoPow#ixzz0pDmFeok3.

Gibran, K. (1923). *The Prophet.* Retrieved 11/9/09 from http://www.katsandogz.com/onjoy.html.

Goettmann, A. (2010). *Dialogue on the Path of Initiation: The Life and Thought of Karlfried Graf Dürckheim.* Trans. T. and R. Nottingham. Retrieved 17/9/10 from http://www.scribd.com/doc/37452385/durckheim.

Grey, M. (1985). *Return from Death.* London: Arkana.

Grof, S. (1993). *The Holotropic Mind.* New York: HarperCollins.

— (2000). *The Psychology of the Future*. Albany: New York Press.

Guji, M. (2005). 'The experience of recovering from terminal cancer.' *Dissertation Abstracts International: Section B: The Sciences and Engineering*, 66(5-B), 2,821.

Haidt, J. (2006). *The Happiness Hypothesis*. London: Arrow.

Han, M. (2006). 'Relationship among perceived parental trauma, attachment and sense of coherence in Southeast Asian American late adolescents.' *Journal of Family Social Work* 9(2), 25–45.

'Happiness is Smile Shaped' (2009). Retrieved 11/3/09 from http://news.bbc.co.uk/1/hi/programmes/happiness_formula/4787558.stm.

Happold, F. C. (1986). *Mysticism*. London: Pelican.

Hardy, A. (1979). *The Spiritual Nature of Man*. Oxford: Clarendon Press.

Hay, D. (1987). *Exploring Inner Space*. Oxford: Mowbray.

Hicks, G. (2007). *One Unknown*. London: Rodale.

Hinchcliffe, K. (2008). 'The sacred addiction: exploring the spiritual and psychological components of Alcoholics Anonymous.' *Journal of Holistic Healthcare* 5(3), 20–25.

Holte, J. C. (1992). *The Conversion Experience in America*. New York: Greenwood.

Huxley, A. (1962). 'Introduction by Aldous Huxley to the Letters of D. H. Lawrence' in *The Letters of D. H. Lawrence* (ed. H. T. Moore), (appendix), 1,247–68. London: Heinemann.

In the Shadow of the Moon (2006) [DVD]. Directed by David Singleton. London: Dox Productions.

Ingram, C. (2003). *Passionate Presence*. New York: Gotham Books.

James, W. (1902/1985). *The Varieties of Religious Experience*. London: Penguin.

Jeffries, S. (2005). 'I have stage four cancer. There is no stage five.' *Guardian*, 12/7/05. Retrieved 1/2/09 from http://www.guardian.co.uk/society/2005/jul/12/books.lifeandhealth.

Johnson, R. C. (1960). *Watcher on the Hills*. New York: Harper.

Kasser. T. (2002). *The High Price of Materialism*. Cambridge, MA: MIT Press.

Kastner, R. S. (1998). 'Beyond breast *cancer* survival: the meaning of thriving.' *Dissertation Abstracts International: Section B: The Sciences and Engineering* 59(5-B), Nov., 2,421.

Kendall-Tackett, K. (2009). 'Psychological trauma and physical health: a psychoneuroimmunology approach to etiology of negative health effects and possible interventions.' *Psychological Trauma: Theory, Research, Practice, and Policy* 1(1), Mar. 2009, 35–48.

Klass, D. (1995). 'Spiritual Aspects of the Resolution of Grief' in H. Wass and R. A. Niemeyer (eds), *Dying: Facing the Facts*. Washington, DC: Taylor and Francis.

Krishnamurti, J. (1926). *The Herald of the Star*. London.

Kübler-Ross, E. (2005). *On Grief and Grieving: Finding the Meaning of Grief through the Five Stages of Loss.* New York: Simon and Schuster.

Kübler-Ross, E., and Kassler, D. (2000). *Life Lessons: How our Mortality Can Teach Us about Life and Living*. London: Simon and Schuster

Lancaster, B. L., and Palframan, J. T. (2009). 'Coping with major life events: the role of spirituality and self-transformation', *Mental Health, Religion and Culture*, 1–20.

Lawrence, D. H. (1993). *Complete Poems*. London: Penguin.

Levine, S. (1997). *A Year to Live*. New York: Three Rivers Press.

Lutyens, M. (1975). *Krishnamurti: The Years of Awakening*, London: John Murray.

— (1983). *Krishnamurti: The Years of Fulfilment*, London: John Murray.

Marriot, E. (2005). 'Starting at the End.' *Observer*, 5/1/05. Retrieved 11/3/09 from http://www.guardian.co.uk/society/2005/may/01/biography.books.

Maslow, A. (1970). *Motivation and Personality* (second edition). New York: Harper and Row.

Massad, S. (2009). 'An Interview with Byron Katie.' Retrieved 13/3/09 from http://www.realization.org/page/doc1/doc107a.htm.

Maxwell, M., and Tschudin, V. (eds) (1990). *Seeing the Invisible: Modern Religious and Other Transcendent Experiences*. London: Penguin.

McDermott, P. (2006). *Pilgrims*. London: Rider.

McNerney, A. (2004). *The Gift of Cancer.* Timonium, MD: Resonant Publishing.

Miller, H. (1965). *Tropic of Cancer*. London: Grafton.

Miller, W. R., and C'de Baca, J. (2001). *Quantum Change*. New York: Guilford Publications.

Moody, R. (1975). *Life After Life*. New York: Bantam Books.

Moore, H. T. (1974). *The Priest of Love*. London: Penguin.

Murtha, W. (2009). *Dying for a Change*. Wichita: Pen and Publish.

Neal, J., Lichtenstein, B., and Banner, D. (1999). 'Spiritual perspectives on individual, organisational and societal transformation.' *Journal of Organisational Change Management* 12(3), 175–85.

Nietzsche, F. (1895). *Nietzsche contra Wagner: Documents of a Psychologist*. Trans. Anthony M. Ludovici. Retrieved 13/8/09 from http://en.wikisource.org/wiki/Nietzsche_contra_Wagner:_Documents_of_a_Psychologist.

Oswald. A., and Blanchflower, D. (2008). 'Is well-being U-shaped over the life cycle?' *Social Science and Medicine* 66(6), 1,733–49.

Oswald, A., and Powdthavee, N. (2008). 'Does happiness adapt? A longitudinal study of disability with implications for economists and judges.' *Journal of Public Economics* 92(5–6), 1,061–77.

Paton, J., Crouch, W., and Camic, P. (2009). 'Young offenders' experiences of traumatic life events: a qualitative investigation.' *Clinical Child Psychology and Psychiatry* 14(1), 43–62.

Paulson, D., and Krippner, S. (2007). *Haunted by Combat*. New York: Praeger.

Pearson, M. L. (1997). 'Childhood trauma, adult trauma, and dissociation.' *Dissociation* 10(1), 58–62.

Philip, C. (2007). 'I jumped and I lived.' *The Times*, 8/2/07. Retrieved 1/2/10 from http://www.timesonline.co.uk/tol/life_and_style/article1348904.ece.

Pyszczynski, T., Greenberg, J., Solomon, S., Arndt, J., and Schimel, J. (2004). 'Why do people need self-esteem? A theoretical and empirical review.' *Psychological Bulletin 130*, 435–68.

Rinpoche, S. (1993). *The Tibetan Book of Living and Dying*. New Delhi: Rupa.

Rosen, D. (1975). 'Suicide survivors: a follow up study of persons who survived jumping from the Golden Gate and San Francisco-Oakland Bridges.' *Western Journal of Medicine* 122(4), 289–94.

Sacks, O. (1990). *Awakenings*. London: Picador.

Satipatthana Sutta (2010). Retrieved 1/2/10 from http://www.accesstoinsight.org/tipitaka/mn/mn.010.nysa.html.

Schulz, R., and Decker, S. (1985). 'Long-term adjustment to physical disability: the role of social support, perceived control and self-blame.' *Journal of Personality and Social Psychology* 48(1), 162–72.

Schwartz, A. (2000). 'The nature of spiritual transformation: a review of the literature.' Retrieved 13/4/09 from http://www.metanexus.net/spiritual_transformation/research/literature_review.

Schweikhart, R. (2009). 'No Frames, No Boundaries: Connecting with the whole planet – from space.' Retrieved 13/9/09 from http://www.context.org/ICLIB/IC03/Schweick.htm.

Seligman, M. (2002). *Authentic Happiness*. New York: Free Press.

Sheikh, A. I., and Marotta, S. A. (2005). 'A cross-validation study of the posttraumatic growth inventory.' *Measurement and Evaluation in Counseling and Development*, *38*(2), 66–77.

Shuchter, S. R. (1986). *Dimensions of Grief: Adjusting to the Death of a Spouse*. San Francisco: Jossey-Bass.

Solomon, S., Greenberg, J., and Pyszczynski, T. (1991). 'A terror management theory of social behavior: the psychological functions of self-esteem and cultural worldviews' in M. P. Zanna (ed.), *Advances in Experimental Social Psychology 24*, 93–159. New York: Academic Press.

'Space: The Greening of the Astronauts' (1972). *Time*, Dec. 11th. Retrieved from http://www.time.com/time/magazine/article/0,9171,878100-3,00.html.

Stanton, A. L., Bower, J. E., and Low, C. A. (2006). 'Posttraumatic Growth after Cancer' in L. Calhoun and R. Tedeschi (eds). *Handbook of Posttraumatic Growth: Research and Practice*. 138–75. Mahwah, NJ: Lawrence Erlbaum Associates.

Taylor, S. (2001). 'Lawrence the Mystic.' *The Journal of the D. H. Lawrence Society*. 62–73. Also available at www.stevenmtaylor.com.

Taylor, S. (2009). 'Spiritual alchemy: when trauma and turmoil lead to the rise of spiritual awakening.' *The Scientific and Medical Network Review*. Winter 2009/10, 11–14.

Tedeschi, R., and Calhoun, L. (1998), *Posttraumatic Growth: Positive Changes in the Aftermath of Crisis.* Mahwah, NJ: Lawrence Erlbaum Associates.

Tedeschi, R., and Calhoun, L. (2004). 'Posttraumatic growth: conceptual foundation and empirical evidence.' *Psychological Inquiry* 15(1), 1–18, 2006.

Tedeschi, R. G., and Calhoun, L. (2004). 'Posttraumatic growth: a new perspective on psychotraumatology.' *Psychiatric Times* 21(4).

Tolle, E. (2001). *The Power of Now*. London: Hodder and Stoughton.

— (2005). *A New Earth*. London: Simon and Schuster.

Tomich, P. L., and Helgeson, V. S. (2004). 'Is finding something good in the bad always good? Benefit finding among women with breast cancer.' *Health Psychology* 23, 16–23.

Tower, D. O. (2000). 'Trans-survivorship: the cancer survivor's journey from trauma to transformation.' *Dissertation Abstracts International: Section B: The Sciences and Engineering* 61(1-B), Jul. 2000, 567.

Underhill, E. (1911/1960). *Mysticism*. London: Methuen.

van der Kolk, B. A., and van der Hart, O. (1989). 'Pierre Janet and the breakdown of adaptation in psychological trauma.' *American Journal of Psychiatry* 146(12), 1,530–40.

Walsh, R., and Vaughan, F. (eds) (1993). *Paths Beyond Ego*. New York: Tarcher/Puttnam.

Wareing, S. (1999). 'Language and Gender' in L. Thomas and S. Wareing (eds), *Language, Society and Power*. London: Routledge.

Watts. A. (1973). *In my Own Way*. London: Cape.

Whitman, W. (1855/1980). *Leaves of Grass*. New York: Penguin.

Whitman, W. (1867). 'To One Shortly to Die.' Retrieved 5/5/10 from http://www.whitmanarchive.org/published/LG/1867/poems/117.

Whitman, W. (1891). 'Whispers of Heavenly Death.' Retrieved 5/5/10 from http://www.whitmanarchive.org/published/LG/1891/clusters/244.

Wilber, K. (1993). *Grace and Grit*. Boston: Shambhala.

— (2000). *One Taste*. Boston: Shambhala.

Zinnbauer, B., and Pargament, K. (1998). 'Spiritual conversion: a study of religious change among college students.' *Journal for the Scientific Study of Religion* 37(1), 161–80.

ACKNOWLEDGEMENTS

First and foremost, I would like to thank all of the shifters who agreed to be interviewed by me for this book and others who wrote descriptions of their awakening experiences (both temporary and permanent): Tracy Caira, Jill Watson, Emma Haughton, Jill Martin, David Keenan, Carrie Mitchell, Cheryl Brown, Iris McCann, Jamie Parham, Janice Hartley, Stephanie Potts, Glyn Hood, Berta Busquet, Claire Sawford (PA to Gill Hicks), Michael Hutchison, Kevin Hinchcliffe, Bob Slater, Eckhart Tolle, Russel Williams, Catherine Ingram, William Murtha, Tony the launderette manager (I never did find out his second name and now his launderette is closed – please contact me, Tony, if you read this book!), Irene Murray, Sandy Geddes, Elizabeth Lake, Stephen Kirk and also several students from my courses on the psychology of happiness at the University of Manchester, whose names I unfortunately didn't keep a record of. All of you were unfailingly generous and completely open, and meeting you all and hearing your stories has enriched my life.

I would like to thank Eckhart Tolle for his support and encouragement over the last five years and also Michelle Pilley, Jessica Crockett and everyone else at Hay House for welcoming me into their fold and believing in my abilities. I am also grateful to Nuria Mustre, who translated Berta's responses to my questions. This book began life as a research project under the supervision of Professor Les Lancaster at Liverpool John Moores University – I would like to thank Les for his guidance and advice.

Finally, I'm very grateful to my old friend Mark Sullivan, for creating and helping me maintain my website, and (im)patiently enduring my technological ineptitude.

FURTHER INFORMATION

For information about Gill Hicks' activities, see www. madforpeace.org and www.walktalk.org.uk. See also Gill's wonderful book *One Unknown* (Rodale, 2007).

For further details on Hugh Martin's transformational experience, see his article 'Reprieve from Death' at www. integralworld.net/martin07.html.

For information about William Murtha, see www. williammurtha.com. See also his inspiring and riveting book, *Dying for a Change* (Pen and Publish, 2009).

For information about Catherine Ingram's books and talks, see www.catherineingram.com.

If you have had an experience similar to those described in this book, please contact me through my website, www.stevenmtaylor.com.

INDEX

Hay House Titles of Related Interest

The Good Retreat Guide,
by Stafford Whiteaker

The Mindful Manifesto,
by Jonty Heaversedge and Ed Halliwell

Shift Happens,
by Robert Holden

When You're Falling, Dive,
by Mark Matousek

Why Kindness Is Good for You,
by David Hamilton

You Know More Than You Think,
by Seka Nikolic

Also available by Steve Taylor

Waking From Sleep

All of the above are available at your local bookshop,
or may be ordered by contacting Hay House.

We hope you enjoyed this Hay House book.
If you would like to receive a free catalogue featuring additional
Hay House books and products, or if you would like information
about the Hay Foundation, please contact:

Hay House UK Ltd
292B Kensal Road • London W10 5BE
Tel: (44) 20 8962 1230; Fax: (44) 20 8962 1239
www.hayhouse.co.uk

***

Published and distributed in the United States of America by:
Hay House, Inc. • PO Box 5100 • Carlsbad, CA 92018-5100
Tel: (1) 760 431 7695 or (1) 800 654 5126;
Fax: (1) 760 431 6948 or (1) 800 650 5115
www.hayhouse.com

***

Published and distributed in Australia by:
Hay House Australia Ltd • 18/36 Ralph Street • Alexandria, NSW 2015
Tel: (61) 2 9669 4299, Fax: (61) 2 9669 4144
www.hayhouse.com.au

***

Published and distributed in the Republic of South Africa by:
Hay House SA (Pty) Ltd • PO Box 990 • Witkoppen 2068
Tel/Fax: (27) 11 467 8904
www.hayhouse.co.za

***

Published and distributed in India by:
Hay House Publishers India • Muskaan Complex • Plot No.3
B-2• Vasant Kunj • New Delhi - 110 070
Tel: (91) 11 41761620; Fax: (91) 11 41761630
www.hayhouse.co.in

***

Distributed in Canada by:
Raincoast • 9050 Shaughnessy St • Vancouver, BC V6P 6E5
Tel: (1) 604 323 7100
Fax: (1) 604 323 2600

***

Sign up via the Hay House UK website to receive the Hay House
online newsletter and stay informed about what's going on with your
favourite authors. You'll receive bimonthly announcements
about discounts and offers, special events, product highlights,
free excerpts, giveaways, and more!
www.hayhouse.co.uk

ABOUT THE AUTHOR

Steve Taylor is an author and lecturer whose main interests are psychology and spirituality. His previous books are *Waking From Sleep*, *The Fall* and *Making Time*. Steve is a lecturer in psychology at Leeds Metropolitan University and a researcher in transpersonal psychology at Liverpool John Moores University. His books have been published in 10 languages, and his essays have been published in over 30 academic journals, magazines and newspapers, including *Psychologies*, *The Daily Express*, *Resurgence*, *The Journal of Consciousness Studies* and *The Journal of Transpersonal Psychology*. His work has been featured widely in the media in the UK, including on BBC Breakfast, BBC World TV, Radio 4 and 5, and in the *Guardian*. He regularly gives talks and lectures, and is a member of the Scientific and Medical Network. Steve lives in Manchester with his wife and three young children.

www.stevenmtaylor.com